Look, Learn & Create

Quilting

A WORKSHOP
101
IN A BOOK

QUARRY

Brimming with creative inspiration, how-to projects, and useful information to enrich your everyday life, Quarto Knows is a favorite destination for those pursuing their interests and passions. Visit our site and dig deeper with our books into your area of interest: Quarto Creates, Quarto Cooks, Quarto Homes, Quarto Lives, Quarto Drives, Quarto Explores, Quarto Gifts, or Quarto Kids.

© 2011 Quarto Publishing Group USA Inc.

This paperback edition published in 2018

First Published in 2011 by Creative Publishing international, an imprint of
The Quarto Group, 100 Cummings Center, Suite 265-D, Beverly, MA 01915, USA.
T (978) 282-9590 F (978) 283-2742
QuartoKnows.com

Quarry Books titles are also available at discount for retail, wholesale, promotional, and bulk purchase. For details, contact the Special Sales Manager by email at specialsales@quarto.com or by mail at The Quarto Group, Attn: Special Sales Manager, 401 Second Avenue North, Suite 310, Minneapolis, MN 55401, USA.

10 9 8 7 6 5 4 3 2 1

ISBN: 978-1-63159-657-5

Digital edition published in 2018
eISBN: 978-1-61059-014-3

Originally found under the following Library of Congress Cataloging-in-Publication Data
Quilting 101 / Editors of Creative Publishing International.
p. cm.
Includes index.
Summary: "Beginner's guide to quilting, teaches all the basic techniques through easy projects".
ISBN-13: 978-1-58923-573-1 (hard cover)
ISBN-10: 1-58923-573-8 (hard cover)
1. Quilting--Technique. I. Creative Publishing International II. Title: Quilting one hundred and one.
TT835.Q489 2011
746.46--dc22
        2010038921

Book Design and Layout: Mighty Media, Inc.
Illustrations: Heather Lambert
Video Script: Cathy Guy
Videographer: Forrest Fox Productions

Printed in China

CONTENTS

How to Use This Book 4

Quilting Basics 6

The Sewing Machine. 8
Machine Accessories. 10
Getting Ready to Sew 12
How to Balance Tension 16
Quilt Seams. 18
Quilting Supplies 20
Fabric Information 25
Selecting the Batting. 30
Rotary Cutting 32
Layering & Basting. 36
Basic Quilting Techniques 40
Binding. 44

Quilting Projects 48

Raw-edge Appliqué Hot Pad 51
Hand Appliquéd Zippered Bag. 57
Quilt-as-you-go Christmas Stocking. 65
Paper-pieced Holiday Coasters. 73
Nine-patch Pillow. 81
Checkerboard Placemats. 87
Double Nine-patch Table Topper. 95
Pieced Sashing Table Runner 103
Flannel Lap Quilt 111
Rail Fence Wall Hanging. 117
Log Cabin Sewing Machine Cover 123
Ohio Star Flange Pillow. 131
Churn Dash Wall Hanging. 139
Flying Geese Doll Blanket 147
Star Sashing Baby Quilt. 155
Bow Ties Wall Hanging. 161

Glossary 168

Patterns. 170

Index 176

How to Use This Book

Welcome to the rewarding world of sewing. Quilting 101 *is designed to encourage creativity and instill confidence as you learn to sew and quilt. Easy-to-follow instructions with colorful photographs and illustrations help you build your sewing skills while making quilted home decorating items and accessories that are as useful as they are appealing.*

Quilting, once a necessary household activity, is now considered an art form. The color combinations and patterns are limited only by your imagination. Many quilters prefer traditional block patterns, but quilts also can be designed in modern, bold, or whimsical styles to complement any décor. If you're learning to sew, quilting is a great way to hone your skills of cutting, piecing, pressing, and stitching with accuracy. And there's no need to purchase expensive fabrics; you may find a purpose for even the smallest pieces of leftover material.

This book will teach you, step-by-step, how to make great-looking quilted items while you're learning the

fundamentals of sewing. The 16 quilting projects provide a sampling of quilt block patterns, techniques, and styles. With each project you'll learn new skills, listed under What You'll Learn.

You will also find tips and explanations throughout the book to help you understand the "why" behind the instructions. And while the projects suggest size and color combinations, the possibilities are endless. Try the variations that accompany some of the projects, or experiment with your own design and fabric choices.

Use the first section of the book to acquaint yourself with the sewing machine and the techniques and supplies you'll need to get started.

Your sewing machine owner's manual is a necessity; refer to it first if you have questions or problems specific to your machine.

Step one of any quilting project is to read the directions thoroughly. Refer to the Quick References for definitions or elaborations on any words or phrases printed **like this** on the page. If the word or phrase is followed by a page number, its reference can be found on the page indicated. At the beginning of every project you will find a list telling you What You'll Need. Read through the information on fabrics before you go shopping so the fabric store will seem a little more user-friendly when you get there.

9 Stitch in the ditch (page 43) on the right side of the quilt, catching the binding on the back of the quilt. Remove the pins as you come to them.

10 Repeat steps 5 to 9 for the lower edge of the quilt. Trim the ends of the upper and lower binding strips even with the edges of the quilt top.

11 Repeat steps 4 to 7 for the sides of the quilt, measuring the quilt top down the middle, from top to bottom, in step 4. Trim the ends of the binding strips to extend ½" (1.3 cm) beyond the finished edges of the quilt.

12 Wrap and pin the binding around the edge, as in step 8. At each end, fold in the raw edges of the binding. Then fold under the ½" (1.3 cm) end; press. Finish wrapping and pinning the binding. Stitch the binding as in step 9.

Quick reference text

Binding a Quilt continued

5 Pin a binding strip on the right side of the upper edge of the quilt, aligning the raw edges of the binding to the raw edge of the quilt top and matching the pin marks. **Insert the pins perpendicular to the raw edges**. The binding will extend 1" (2.5 cm) beyond the quilt at each end.

6 Stitch the binding strip to the quilt ¼" (6 mm) from the raw edges of the binding. **Remove the pins as you come to them**.

7 Trim off the excess batting and backing ½" (1.3 cm) from the stitching line.

8 Wrap the binding snugly around the edge of the quilt, covering the stitching line on the back of the quilt. Pin the binding in place from the right side, inserting the pins parallel to the binding in the seam "ditch" and catching the folded edge on the back. For easy removal, insert all the pins so that the heads will be toward you when you are stitching.

QUICK REFERENCE

Insert the pins perpendicular to the raw edges. This makes it easier to remove them as you sew. The pin heads are near the raw edge where you can grasp them with your right hand. In this position, you are much less likely to stick yourself with a pin as you sew.

Remove pins as you come to them. As tempting as it may be, don't sew over pins! You may be lucky and save a few seconds, or you could hit a pin and break your needle, costing you much more time in the long run.

Quick reference

The online videos associated with this book will show you the essential techniques used for quilting. To access the online videos, visit **www.creativepub.com/pages/quilting-101**. Most of all, have fun with these quilting projects! Enjoy the creative process while you learn new skills.

Quilting Basics

This book is written for the beginning quilter, but not everyone starts from the same place. Some beginners have sewing skills but have never sewn a quilt. Others have never sewn a stitch but quilting is where they want to begin. For someone new to quilting, even a trip to the quilt shop or fabric store can be challenging. Manufacturers can't include all the vital information with their packaging, and there are so many tools and quilting notions to choose from. To give you a firm foundation for learning to quilt, this section teaches you the essentials about your sewing machine, fabrics, sewing and quilting supplies, and specific quilting techniques. If you have never taken a stitch, you will appreciate the detailed information, photos, and illustrations. Even if you have sewing or quilting experience, you are sure to learn some things you didn't know. So settle back, take your time, and jump into the basics.

The Sewing Machine

The principle parts common to all modern sewing machines are shown and listed at right. The parts may look different on your model, and they may have slightly different locations, so open your owner's manual also. If you do not have an owner's manual for your machine, you should be able to get one from a sewing machine dealer who sells your brand. Become familiar with the names of the parts and their functions. As you spend more time sewing, these items will become second nature to you.

If you are buying a new machine, consider how much and what kind of sewing you expect to do. Talk to friends who sew and to sales personnel. Ask for demonstrations, and sew on the machine yourself. Experiment with the various features while sewing on a variety of fabrics, including knits, wovens, lightweights, and denim. Think about the optional features of the machine and which ones you want on yours. Leading sewing machine manufacturers offer a variety of models, including some that are specifically designed for machine quilting. You can, of course, do other kinds of sewing on these machines but they may have special features like a deeper bed to accommodate bulky layers for quilting, specialized feed systems, special presser feet for sewing accurate seams, and automatic stitch regulators to ensure even quilting stitches. Many dealers offer free sewing lessons with the purchase of a machine. Take advantage! These lessons will be geared to your particular brand and model of sewing machine.

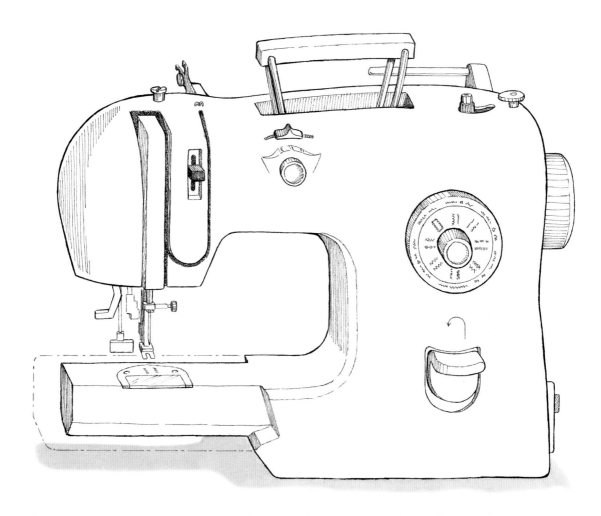

These parts are common to all sewing machines, but their position and design differs. Use your manual to help you learn where these parts are, what these parts do, and how to use them:

Bobbin
Bobbin case
Bobbin winder spindle
Bobbin winder tension
Buttonhole knob
Detachable machine bed
Feed dogs
Feed dog control
General-purpose presser foot
Handwheel
Light switch
Needle clamp
Presser foot lifter

Presser foot pressure control
Spool pins
Stitch pattern selector
Stitch length selector
Stitch width selector
Take-up lever
Top tension control
Top tension discs
Thread cutter
Thread guides
Throat plate
Variable speed switch

Machine Accessories

Sewing Machine Needles

Sewing machine needles come in a variety of styles and sizes. The correct needle choice depends mostly on the fabric you have selected. Sharp points (A), used for woven fabrics, are designed to pierce the fabric. Ballpoints (B) are designed to slip between the loops of knit fabric rather than pierce and possibly damage the fabric. Universal points are designed to work on both woven and knitted fabrics. The size of the needle is designated by a number, generally given in both European (60, 70, 80, 90, 100, 110) and American (9, 11, 12, 14, 16, 18) numbering systems. Use size 11/70 or 12/80 needles for medium-weight fabrics. A larger number means the needle is thicker and that it is appropriate for use with heavier fabrics and heavier threads.

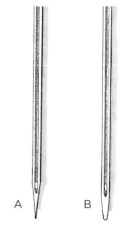

A   B

Bobbins

Stitches are made by locking the upper thread with a lower thread, carried on a bobbin. Always use bobbins in the correct style and size for your machine. Bobbin thread tension is controlled by a spring on the bobbin case, which may be built in (A) or removable (B).

TIP Though needle style and size are usually indicated in some way on the needle, it is often difficult to see without a magnifying glass, and you most likely will not remember what needle is in the machine. As an easy reminder, when you finish a sewing session, leave a fabric swatch from your current project under the presser foot.

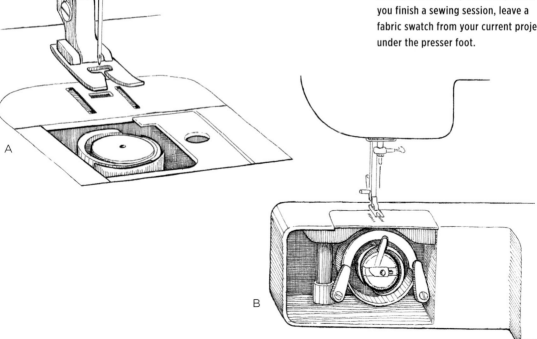

Presser Feet

Every sewing machine comes with accessories for specialized tasks. More can be purchased as you develop your interest and skills. Your machine manual or dealer can show you what accessories are available and will explain how to use them to get the best results.

A general-purpose foot (A), probably the one you will use most often, has a wide opening to accommodate the side-to-side movement of the needle in all types of utility (nondecorative) stitches. It is also suitable for most straight stitching. A quarter-inch presser foot (B) aligns to the edge of the fabric to sew perfect ¼" (6 mm) seams, just right for piecing quilt blocks. A special-purpose or embroidery foot (C) has a grooved bottom that allows the foot to ride smoothly over decorative stitches or raised cords. Some styles have a wide space between the toes; others are clear plastic, allowing you to see your work more clearly. A walking foot (D) feeds top and bottom layers at equal rates, allowing you to more easily match patterns or stitch bulky layers, as in quilted projects. A zipper foot (E) is used to insert zippers or to stitch any seam that has more bulk on one side than the other. For some sewing machines, the zipper foot is stationary, requiring you to move the needle position to the right or left. For other styles, the position of the zipper foot itself is adjustable.

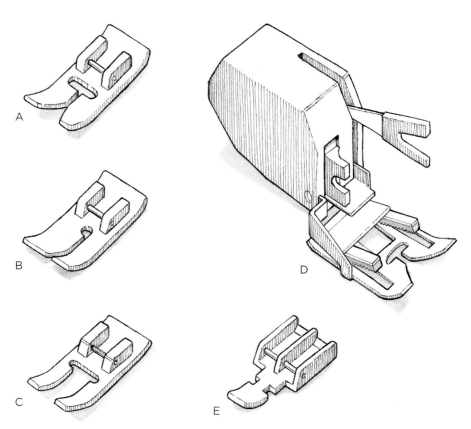

Getting Ready to Sew

Simple tasks of inserting the needle, winding the bobbin, and threading the machine have tremendous influence on the stitch quality and performance of your machine. Use this guide as a general reference, but refer to your owner's manual for instructions specific to your machine.

Inserting the Needle

Loosen the needle clamp. After selecting the appropriate needle for your project (page 10), insert it into the machine as high as it will go. The grooved side of the needle faces forward if your bobbin gets inserted from the front or top; it faces to the left if your bobbin gets inserted on the left. Tighten the clamp securely.

Winding the Bobbin

If the bobbin case is built in, the bobbin is wound in place with the machine fully threaded as if to sew (page 14).

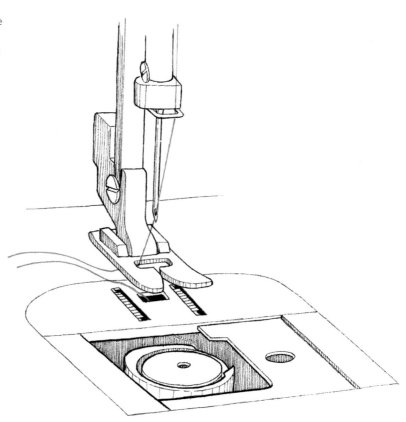

Removable bobbins are wound on the top or side of the machine, with the machine threaded for bobbin winding, as described in your owner's manual.

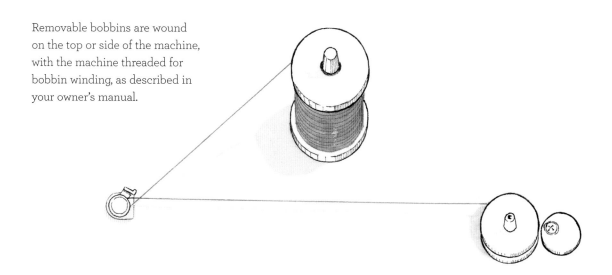

Bobbin thread must be drawn through the bobbin case tension spring. For wind-in-place bobbins, this happens automatically when you wind the bobbin, but you must do it manually when you insert a bobbin that already has thread on it.

After inserting the bobbin and threading the machine (page 14), you need to draw the bobbin thread to the top. Hold the needle thread while turning the handwheel toward you one full turn. As the needle goes down, the top thread interlocks with the bobbin thread and brings it up through the needle hole. Pull both threads together under the presser foot and off to the side or back.

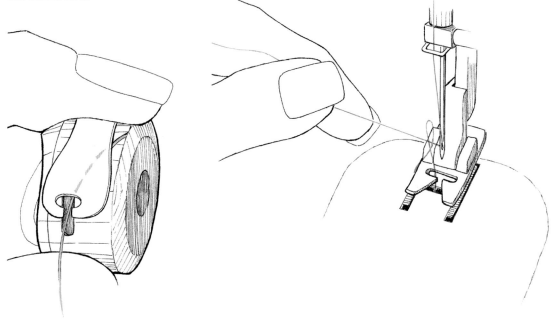

Threading the Machine

Because every sewing machine is different, the threading procedure for your machine may differ slightly from the one shown here. Once again, it is important to refer to your owner's manual. Every upper thread guide adds a little tension to the thread as it winds its way to the needle. Missing one of them can make a big difference in the quality of your stitches.

1 Set the thread spool on the spindle. For a vertical spindle, position the spool so that it will turn clockwise as you sew. If the spindle is horizontal, the spool is held in place with an end cap. If your spool has a small cut in one end for minding the thread, position the spool with that end to the right.

TIP If the spool is new and has paper labels covering the holes, poke them in, completely uncovering the holes, to allow the spool to turn freely.

Unless your machine has a self-winding bobbin, you will want to wind the bobbin (page 13) before threading the machine.

2 Pull thread to the left and through the first thread guide

3 Draw thread through the tension guide.

TIP It is very important to have the presser foot lever up when threading the machine because the tension discs are then open. If the presser foot is down and the discs are closed, the thread will not slide between the discs, and your stitches will not make you happy.

4 Draw thread through the next thread guide.

5 Insert thread through the take-up lever.

6 Draw the thread through the remaining thread guides.

7 Thread the needle. Most needles are threaded from front to back; some, from left to right.

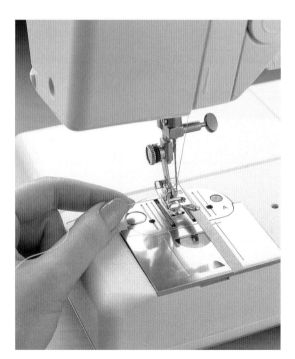

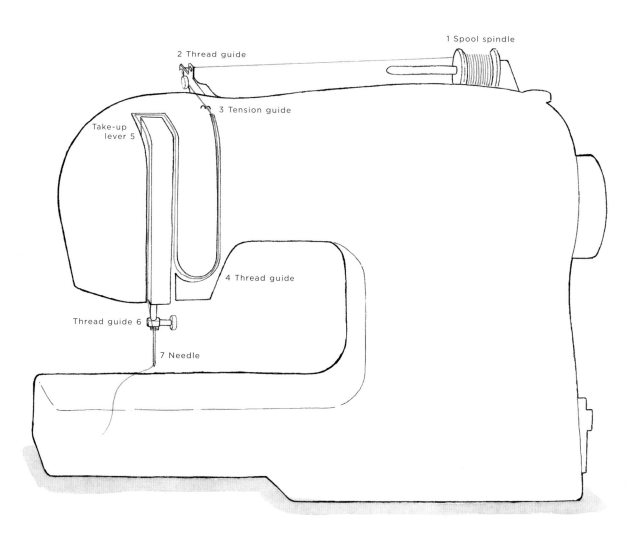

1 Spool spindle

2 Thread guide

3 Tension guide

Take-up lever 5

4 Thread guide

Thread guide 6

7 Needle

How to Balance Tension

Your machine forms stitches by interlocking the bobbin thread with the needle thread. Every time the needle goes down into the fabric, a sharp hook catches the needle thread and wraps the bobbin thread around it. Imagine this little tug-of-war. If the needle thread tension is "stronger" than the bobbin thread tension, the needle thread pulls the bobbin thread through to the top. If the bobbin thread tension is "stronger," it pulls the needle thread through to the bottom. When the tensions are evenly balanced, the stitch will lock exactly halfway between the top and bottom of the layers being sewn, which is right where you want it.

Some machines have "self-adjusting tension," meaning the machine automatically adjusts its tension with every fabric you sew. For machines that do not have this feature, you may have to adjust the needle thread tension slightly as you sew different fabrics.

Testing the Tension

1 Thread your machine and insert the bobbin, using two very different colors of thread, neither of which matches the fabric. Cut an 8" (20.5 cm) square of a smooth, mediumweight fabric. Fold the fabric in half diagonally, and place it under the presser foot so the fold aligns to your ½" (1.3 cm) seam guide. Lower the presser foot and set your stitch length at ten stitches per inch or 2.5 mm long.

2 Stitch a line across the fabric, stitching ½" (1.3 cm) from the diagonal fold. Remove the fabric from the machine. Inspect your stitching line from both sides. If your tension is evenly balanced, you will see only one color on each side. If you see both thread colors on the top side of your sample, the needle tension is tighter than the bobbin tension. If you see both thread colors on the back side of your sample, the bobbin tension is tighter than the needle tension.

3 Pull on your stitching line until you hear threads break. (Because you stitched on the BIAS, the fabric will stretch slightly.) If the thread breaks on only one side, your machine's tension is tighter on that side.

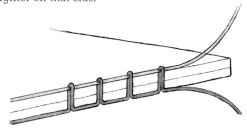

Top tension too tight

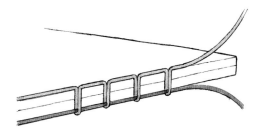

Top tension too loose

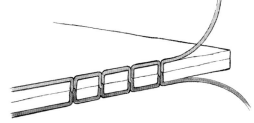

Tensions even

Adjusting the Tension

Before adjusting the tension on your machine, first check:

- that your machine is properly threaded (page 14)
- that your bobbin is properly installed
- that your needle is not damaged and is inserted correctly

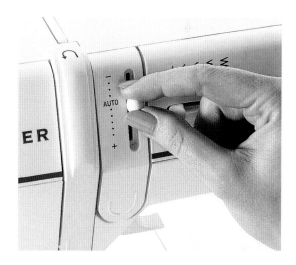

After checking these three things, you may need to adjust the tension on your machine. (Check your owner's manual.) Tighten or loosen the needle thread tension slightly to bring the needle thread and bobbin thread tensions into balance. Test the stitches after each adjustment, until you achieve balanced tension. If slight adjustments of the needle tension dial do not solve the problem, the bobbin tension may need adjusting. However, most manufacturers do not recommend that you adjust bobbin tension yourself, so unless you have received instructions for adjusting the bobbin tension on your machine, take your machine in for repair.

Quilt Seams

Quilting is like putting puzzles together. Lots of squares, rectangles, triangles, and fabric strips are pieced together to make a colorful fabric picture.

Every seam is sewn using ¼" (6 mm) seam allowances. In order to make all the pieces fit precisely, you must sew every seam accurately. Most machines have a seam allowance guide on the throat plate; however, it may not include a mark for ¼" (6 mm). Often, the distance from the needle tip to the edge of the presser foot is exactly ¼" (6 mm). If neither of these guides works for your machine, mark a ¼" (6 mm) seam guide on the bed of your machine with tape.

Making a Seam Guide

Mark a line ¼" (6 mm) from the edge on a small square of fabric. Put the fabric under the presser foot, so that the marked line aligns to the tip of the needle. Place tape on the bed of the machine even with the cut edge of the fabric. Use the tape as a guide for sewing all your seams.

Sewing Seams

1 Thread your machine (page 14) and insert the bobbin (page 13). Holding the needle thread with your left hand, turn the handwheel toward you until the needle has gone down and come back up to its highest point. A stitch will form, and you will feel a tug on the needle thread. Pull on the needle thread to bring the bobbin thread up through the hole in the throat plate. Pull both threads together under the presser foot and off to one side.

TIP Straight stitching lines are easier to achieve if you watch the edge of the fabric along the seam guide and ignore the needle. Sew smoothly at a relaxing pace, with minimal starting and stopping and without bursts of speed. You have better control of the speed if you operate your foot control with your heel resting on the floor.

2 Place two fabric squares right sides together, aligning the outer edges. Pin the pieces together along one long edge, inserting the pins perpendicular to the edge. Place the fabric under the presser foot so the pinned side edges align to the ¼" (6 mm) seam guide and the upper edges align to the needle hole in the throat plate. Lower the presser foot, and set your stitch length at 2 mm, which equals 15 stitches per inch.

3 Begin stitching slowly. Hold the thread tails under a finger for the first few stitches. This prevents the needle thread from being pulled out of the needle and also prevents the thread tails from being drawn down into the bobbin case, where they could potentially cause the dreaded *thread jam*. Gently guide the fabric while you sew by walking your fingers ahead of and slightly to the sides of the presser foot. Remember, you are only guiding; let the machine pull the fabric.

4 Stop stitching and remove pins as you come to them. When you reach the end of the fabric, stop again. Turn the handwheel toward you until the needle is in its highest position.

5 Raise the presser foot. Pull the fabric smoothly away from the presser foot, either to the left side or straight back. If you have to tug the threads, turn your handwheel slightly toward you until they pull easily. Cut the threads, leaving tails on the fabric and coming from the machine.

QUICK REFERENCE

Thread jam. No matter how conscientious you are at trying to prevent them, thread jams just seem to be lurking out there waiting to mess up your day. DON'T USE FORCE! Remove the presser foot, if you can. Snip all the threads you can get at from the top of the throat plate. Open the bobbin case door or throat plate, and snip any threads you can get at. Remove the bobbin, if you can. Gently remove the fabric. Thoroughly clean out the feed dog and bobbin area before reinserting the bobbin and starting over. Then just chalk it up to experience and get over it!

Quilting Supplies

The process of quilting involves several basic tasks: measuring, cutting, marking, and stitching. For each of these steps there are special tools and supplies to save you time, improve your accuracy, and make the project go smoothly.

Measuring & Cutting Tools

Buy quality cutting tools and use them only for sewing! Cutting paper and other non-fabric materials will dull your tools quickly. Sharp tools make precise cuts easier and, in the long run, will save you time.

Rotary cutters (A) allow you to cut smooth edges on multiple layers of fabric quickly and easily. The cutters are available in different sizes. Small cutters work well for curves and a few layers of fabric; the larger ones are ideal for long straight lines and many layers of fabric.

Cutting mats (B), made especially for use with rotary cutters, protect your blade and table top. Mats come in a variety of sizes. Choose one at least 22" (56 cm) wide to accommodate a width of fabric folded in half. A mat with a printed grid is a useful guide for cutting right angles.

You'll want a clear quilting ruler (C) to use as a measuring tool and as a guide for your rotary cutter. A ruler 6" × 24" (15 × 61 cm) is a popular, versatile size. Square rulers and rulers with 30°, 45°, and 60° angle lines also are available.

Sewing scissors (D) and shears (E) are sewing necessities. Purchase the best quality you can afford.

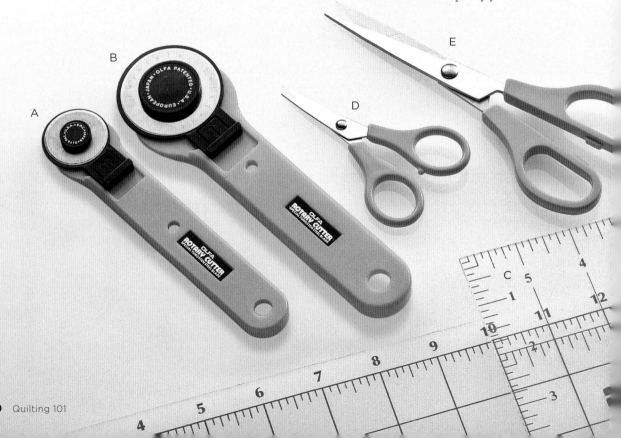

Marking Tools

The marks you make on fabric should last only as long as you need them. You should be able to remove them easily without damaging the quilt. Always test a marker on a sample swatch of fabric first and remember to mark lightly!

A special fabric eraser (F) can be used to remove light lead pencil marks without damaging fabric. Quilter's pencils (G), available in white or gray lead, have eraser ends for easy removal. The leads are oil-free and contain less graphite to prevent smearing. Soapstone pencils (H), made of pressed talc, can be sharpened to a fine point and rubbed off or wiped with a damp cloth. Water-soluble pencils (I), handy for marking on darker fabrics, can be removed with a damp cloth.

Pins, Needles & Thread

Quilting pins (A), used for pinning your pieces together, are 1¾" (4.5 cm) long and have large glass heads.

Curved, rustproof safety pins (B) in 1" to 1½" (2.5 to 3.8 cm) size make quick work of basting your quilting projects.

Milliner's needles (C) with small, round eyes are preferred by quilters who want to hand-baste the layers together.

Betweens (D) are short needles with round eyes for sewing small hand-quilting stitches. Sharps, similar to betweens but slightly longer, are used for appliquéing and general hand sewing.

Cotton-covered polyester threads and 100% cotton threads (E) are available for machine and hand quilting. Hand-quilting threads have a polished glacé finish that provides abrasion resistance and prevents tangling and knotting; 100% cotton basting thread is also available.

Fine monofilament thread (F) can also be used for machine quilting, making the stitches less noticeable.

Pressing Equipment & Techniques

Pressing at each stage of construction is the secret to perfect piecing. The general rule is to press each stitched seam before crossing it with another. Often you can sew the same seam in numerous sets before making the trip to the ironing board to press them all.

Pressing your seams carefully is crucial to your success, second only to accurate sewing of the ¼" (6 mm) seams. Use the tip of the iron, moving only in the direction of the grainlines. Be especially cautious when pressing seams sewn on the bias. Careless pressing can distort the shape and size of your quilt project. Both seam allowances are usually pressed together to one side or the other. Following the pressing plan in the project directions will help you produce a neat, precise design.

Use a steam/spray iron with a wide temperature range. Buy a dependable, name-brand iron. Because your iron will be left on and standing still for several minutes between pressing steps, avoid an iron with an automatic shut-off feature.

An ironing board provides a sufficient surface for pressing, but you may want to invest in a fold-out surface, such as the Spaceboard, shown. It has a cotton cover printed with a measured grid to help you press your pieces more accurately.

Fabric Information

After you have chosen a quilt design, it's time to select the fabric. This may seem like a difficult task at first, but consider it an adventure and have fun. This is the time to use your vision and creativity. Just as two painters can paint the same landscape and produce very different effects, your choice of patterns, colors, and the way you combine them will give each project your unique style.

Fabrics made of 100% cotton or cotton blends can be used. Both are available in a wide variety of patterns and colors, so you'll have plenty of options to choose from. Many quilters prefer using 100% cotton fabrics because they find them easier to sew, press, mark, and hand-quilt.

If you are shopping for your fabrics in a quilt shop, they will probably be arranged according to their colors or print types, and you'll rarely find fabric that is not pure cotton. In a general fabric store, you may find a section for quilting fabrics, but there are probably other suitable fabrics located elsewhere in the store. Be sure to check the labels for fiber content and care.

The outer edges of woven fabrics are called selvages. As a general rule, they should be trimmed away (page 33), because they are more tightly woven than the rest of the fabric, and they may shrink when laundered or pressed. Grainlines are the directions in which the fabric yarns run. Strong, stable, lengthwise yarns, running parallel to the selvages, form the lengthwise grain. The crosswise grain is perpendicular to the lengthwise grain and has a small amount of give. The diagonal direction, which has considerable stretch, is called the bias.

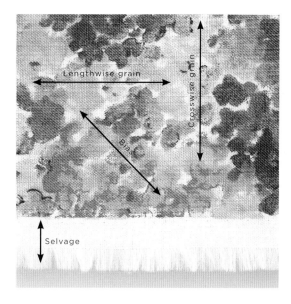

Prints

Printed cotton fabrics are available in a wide range of design styles and print sizes. They include batiks, homespun plaids and florals, tiny-grained prints that "read" as solids, reproduction prints reminiscent of the 1930s, and soft flannels.

Solids

Solid-color fabrics come in a rainbow of colors, with shades and tints to suit any purpose. They include a variety of hand-dyed cottons that have a subtle sueded look. You'll often find them in packets of graduated color values or hues. Muslin, available bleached or unbleached, is usually used for the background pieces in a design, for plain blocks, or for the quilt backing.

Backing Fabrics

The backing fabric should have the same care requirements as the fabrics in the quilt top. For smaller projects, especially when the backing is visible, back the quilt top with one of the fabrics used on the front. For wall hangings and other items where the backing is rarely seen, muslin is a good choice. If you want to accentuate the quilting stitches on the backing side, choose a solid-colored fabric. Printed fabrics tend to hide the stitches.

Preparing the Fabric

Preshrink your fabric, especially if you intend to launder the finished project. Most cotton fabrics shrink 2 to 3 percent when washed and dried, so if they're not preshrunk, the fabrics may pucker at the stitching lines and the finished size of the quilted piece may change the first time it is washed.

Launder fabrics in your washing machine on a short, warm cycle. There's no need to use detergent, but be sure to wash like colors together in case they aren't colorfast. Check the rinse water of dark or vivid fabrics to be sure they are colorfast; if dye transfers to the water, continue rinsing the fabric until the water is clear. Machine dry the fabric until it is only slightly damp, and then press it.

Selecting Fabrics

Use contrasting colors to make the pieces of a quilt block stand out from each other. Combine warm colors (reds, yellows, or oranges) in the same quilt block with cool colors (blues, greens, or violets) to make them all seem more vivid, as shown in the Log Cabin block (at right).

Any fabric shape, whether solid-color or print, will "pop" from the quilt surface when surrounded by white or nearly white fabric. This is readily apparent in the blue and white Ohio Star block (below).

Select a multicolor print first, perhaps for the border. Then select fabrics for the quilt block pieces, drawing colors from the print, as shown in the Ohio Star pillow (at left).

Interesting visual effects are achieved by using colors with graduated values (lightness or darkness). Stack all the fabrics you are considering on a table; then stand back and squint. Or view them through a special filtering tool, available at quilt shops, designed for judging color values. The filter blocks out color and reveals only the lightness or darkness of the fabric.

Combine fabrics with various print scales and styles to add visual texture to your quilt. Don't be afraid to cut up a large-scale print into smaller pieces.

Selecting the Batting

The middle layer of the quilt is called the batting. When selecting batting for any project, consider the amount of loft, its drapability, and the distance required between quilting stitches to prevent the batting from bunching or pulling apart. This distance, usually ranging from 1" to 6" (2.5 to 15 cm), is printed on the package label.

Cotton, polyester, and cotton/polyester blends are the most common fibers used in batting. Cotton batting gives a flat, traditional appearance when quilted. It absorbs moisture and is cool in the summer and warm in the winter. Polyester batting is more durable, is easier to handle than cotton, and gives a slightly puffier look. It provides warmth without weight, is nonallergenic, and resists moth and mildew damage. For the traditional appearance of cotton, but the stability and ease in handling of polyester, choose a cotton/polyester blend.

Low-loft battings are recommended for machine quilting but even low-loft battings vary in thickness. Extra-low-loft battings are often used for garments or placemats. For wall hangings or lap quilts, select a low-loft batting that is sturdy but drapable.

Batting is available in a wide range of sizes, although the selection in certain fibers and construction types may be limited. Available in quilting stores and many fabric stores, batting can be purchased by the yard and in small packages for clothing and craft projects. It is also packaged for standard-size bed quilts.

Low-loft polyester batting, used in this wall hanging, is easy to machine-quilt and very durable.

Cotton/polyester low-loft batting provides warmth, durability, and easy laundering for a cozy lap quilt.

Extra-low-loft polyester batting is a good choice for placemats or table runners, when you want a subtle quilted look for an item that may be laundered often.

Rotary Cutting

Accuracy in cutting is critical to successful quilting. A small error, multiplied by each piece, will result in blocks that don't fit together. You don't need that kind of frustration when you are learning to quilt! Take the time to cut accurately, and give yourself a head start in the quilting game.

You'll find the investment in a rotary cutter and mat well worth it, once you start to use them. While indispensable for quilting, they are also perfectly suited for many other sewing projects. Rotary cutting is not only a very accurate method, it also saves time. Instead of cutting each piece of the quilt individually, you can cut several identical pieces at once and have the entire project cut and ready to sew in minutes.

Straightening the Fabric

1 First, determine the grainline. Fold the fabric in half and hold it by the selvages. Shift one side, if necessary, until the fabric hangs straight. The foldline is the straight lengthwise grain.

2 Lay the fabric on the cutting mat, with the fold along a grid line. Place the ruler on the fabric, close to the raw edge, at a 90° angle to the fold. Holding the ruler firmly in place with one hand, trim the excess fabric off along the edge of the ruler, using the rotary cutter. Apply steady, firm pressure to the blade. Stop when the rotary cutter gets past your hand.

3 Leave the blade in position, and reposition your hand on the ruler ahead of the blade. Hold firmly, and continue cutting. Make sure the fabric and the ruler don't move. Shift your hand position on the ruler whenever necessary.

4 Reposition the folded fabric on the cutting mat with the straightened end on a horizontal grid line. Place the ruler over the fabric perpendicular to the cut end, with the edge just inside the selvages. Cut off the selvages, using the rotary cutter as in steps 2 and 3.

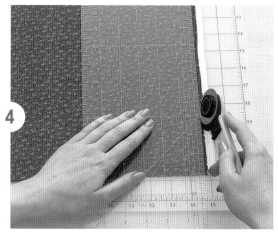

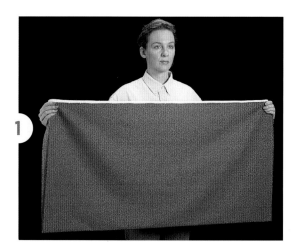

Cutting Strips

1 Position the folded fabric so that the edge you will be cutting is on the left if you are right-handed, or on the right if you are left-handed. Place the ruler on the fabric, aligning the trimmed edge with the appropriate measurement on the ruler. Holding the ruler firmly, cut as on page 33, steps 2 and 3.

2 Lift the ruler and move the cut strip so that you are able to see the cutting line. Reposition the ruler and cut the next strip.

TIP These photos show you how a right-handed person would hold the ruler and rotary cutter. If you are left-handed, you would hold the tools in opposite hands and work from the opposite direction.

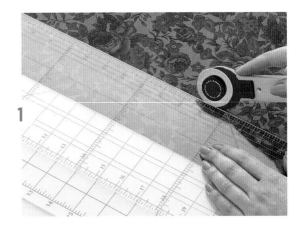

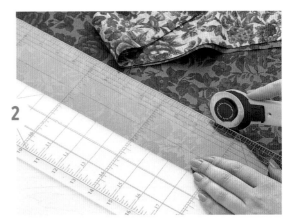

Cutting Squares or Rectangles

Stack three or four strips, matching the edges exactly. Place the ruler on the fabric, aligning the short edge of the fabric with the appropriate measurement on the ruler. Hold the ruler firmly in place. Cut the fabric, guiding the rotary cutter along the edge of the ruler.

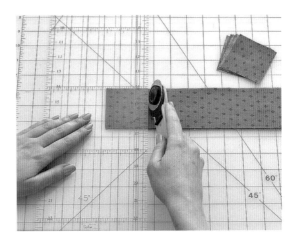

Cutting Triangles

Stack three or four squares, matching the edges exactly. Place the ruler over the squares diagonally, aligning it exactly to the corners of the squares. Cut through the squares, guiding the rotary cutter along the edge of the ruler. The project directions will tell you what size to cut the squares and whether to cut them diagonally once or twice.

TIP Because rotary cutters are extremely sharp, the manufacturers have designed ways to cover or retract the blades. Always use this safety feature every time you put the tool down. An open blade falling from a table can easily slice through leather shoes. Keep your fingers out of the way when you are cutting, avoiding awkward positions where you have less control. Above all, keep the cutters in a safe place where children will not find them.

Cutting a Rectangle Wider than the Ruler

1 Measure the width of the strip in from the cut edge in several places; mark the fabric, using chalk or a pencil.

2 Align the ruler to the marks, and hold it firmly in place. Cut the fabric, guiding the rotary cutter along the edge of the ruler over the marks.

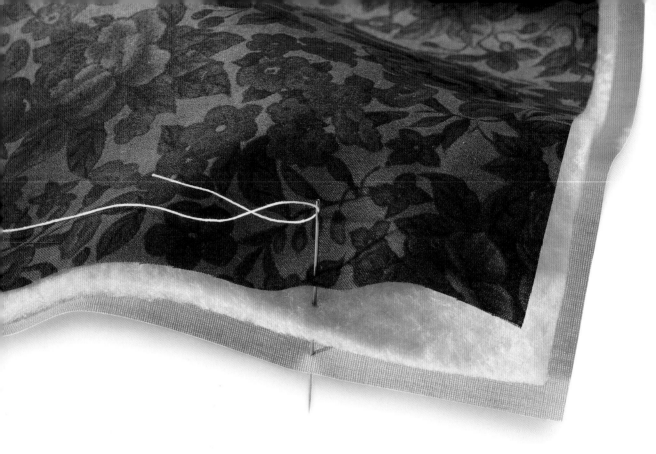

Layering & Basting

Every quilt project, from the simplest one-piece hot pad to a multi-block bed quilt, must be layered and basted before you proceed with the actual quilting stitches. Basting keeps the quilt top, batting, and backing from shifting while you are quilting.

Traditionally, quilts have been basted using a hand needle and thread. While this is still a viable alternative, you may save a little time basting with safety pins. If you prefer basting with thread, use a single strand of white cotton thread and a large milliner's or darning needle. For safety-pin basting, use only rust-proof pins in either 1" or 1½" (2.5 or 3.8 cm) size. Special quilter's safety pins are bent for easier insertion. For either method, follow the same steps for layering the quilt.

Layering the Quilt

1 Press the quilt top and backing fabric flat. Mark the center of each side of the quilt top at the raw edges, using safety pins. Repeat this step for the batting and the backing. Place the backing on your work surface, wrong side up. Use masking tape to tape the backing securely to your work surface, beginning at the center of each side and working toward the corners. Keep the fabric taut but not stretched.

2 Place the batting on the backing, matching the center pins on all sides. Smooth the batting (but don't stretch it), working from the center of the quilt out to the sides.

3 Place the quilt top, right side up, over the batting, matching the pins on each side. Again, smooth the fabric without stretching it. For clarity, the photos show a solid piece of fabric in place of a multicolor pieced quilt top.

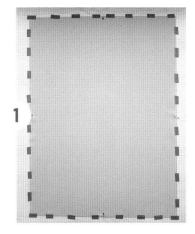

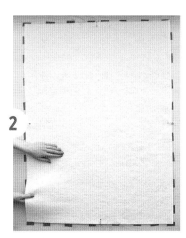

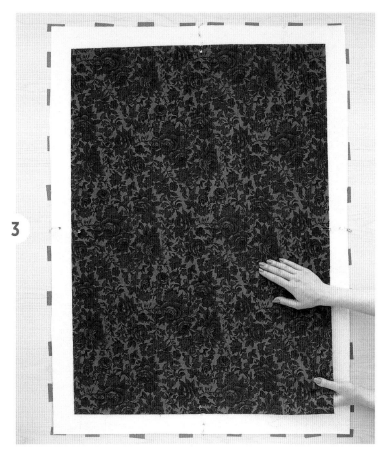

Basting with Thread

1 Thread the needle with a long strand of thread; tie a knot in the end. Begin at the center of the quilt, and stitch toward the side, taking 1" (2.5 cm) stitches through all three layers. Avoid stitching directly on seamlines or marked quilting lines. Pull the stitches snug so the layers will not shift.

2 Baste to the side of the quilt. **_Backstitch_** two or three stitches to secure.

3 Repeat steps 1 and 2 in each direction, so that you have divided the quilt into four quadrants with the basting stitches.

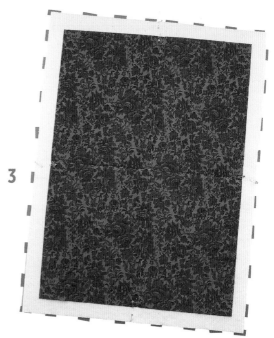

TIP As you run out of thread, backstitch a few stitches. Then rethread the needle, knot the thread, and continue basting from where you stopped.

QUICK REFERENCE

Backstitch. Take a few stitches in the opposite direction when you get to the end of a basting row. This will hold the basting in place but is easier to remove than a knot.

4 Baste parallel rows of stitches, no less than 6" (15 cm) apart, in one quadrant of the quilt. Work from the existing basting line toward the outer edge. Then repeat with parallel rows in the opposite direction.

5 Repeat step 4 for each quadrant of the quilt. Remove the tape from the backing. Fold the edges of the backing over the batting and edges of the quilt top, and safety-pin them in place. This prevents the raw edges from raveling and prevents the batting from catching on the needle and feed dogs during quilting.

Basting with safety pins

Follow the same guidelines, first dividing the quilt into quadrants, and then working on one quadrant at a time. Insert all the pins in the same direction. Space them no more than 6" (15 cm) apart in parallel rows, vertically and horizontally. Avoid placing pins where you will be quilting.

TIP Safety-pin basting goes more quickly if the pins are all open. In fact, they can be purchased at quilting stores already opened. Then, as you remove them from your quilt, leave them open and ready for the next project. You'll save a little wear and tear on your fingers.

Basic Quilting Techniques

Quilting stitches hold the quilt top, batting, and backing of the quilt together. But beyond its function, quilting adds texture and interest to the quilt, enhancing its pieced design. For best effect, the quilting should reinforce or complement the piecing or appliqué design, and it should form an appealing design on the back as well as the front of the quilt.

You can quilt by hand or by machine; there are advantages to either method. Hand quilting is the traditional method, and many quilters still prefer it that way. Machine quilting, of course, takes less time and is also more durable. Whether quilting by hand or machine, your stitching should cover the surface of the quilt uniformly. This guideline is more than just an aesthetic consideration; heavily quilted areas tend to shrink more than lightly quilted areas.

WHAT YOU'LL NEED . . . .

FOR HAND QUILTING:

- Hand-quilting thread
- Between or sharp hand needle (page 22)
- Thimble
- Quilting hoop

FOR MACHINE QUILTING:

- Walking foot
- All-purpose thread or nylon monofilament thread

Hand Quilting

1 Center the area you will work on in your quilting hoop. Thread a between or sharp needle with a single strand of hand-quilting thread, about 18" (46 cm) long; tie a small knot in the end. Take one long stitch, inserting the needle from the front into the batting, about 1" (2.5 cm) from where you want to begin stitching. Don't stitch through to the backing. Bring the needle up where you will begin quilting.

2 Pull on your thread, gently "popping" the knot under the surface of the fabric. Don't pull too hard, or you'll pull the stitch out completely.

3 Take small, even stitches, up and down, through all three layers. If possible, take two to four stitches on your needle before pulling it through the quilt. Strive for quilting that looks the same on the front and the back of the quilt. The stitches should be the same length on both sides.

TIP To avoid poking a hole in the finger that pushes the needle, you'll want to wear a thimble. Many quilters find leather thimbles more comfortable than plastic or metal.

4 To finish a row of quilting, tie a small knot close to the surface of the fabric next to your last stitch. Use your thumbnail to gently pull the fabric, again "popping" the knot under the surface of the fabric. Take a shallow stitch, and clip the thread.

TIP While small stitches are desirable, uniformity is more important. Practice taking six stitches per inch (2.5 cm) as a beginner.

Machine Quilting

1 Attach a walking foot (page 11). Place the quilt under the foot, in the area where you will begin quilting. Lower the foot. Turn the handwheel by hand for one stitch, and stop with the needle at the highest position. Raise the foot, and pull on the needle thread to bring the bobbin thread up through the fabric.

2 Draw both threads under the walking foot to one side. Lower the walking foot, with the needle aligned to enter the fabric at the desired starting point.

3 Stitch several very short stitches to secure the threads at the beginning of the stitching line. Gradually increase the stitch length for about ½" (1.3 cm), until it is the desired length; about 15 stitches per inch, which equals 2 mm.

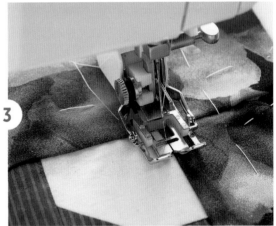

4 Slow your stitching as you approach a stopping point. Beginning about ½" (1.3 cm) from the end, gradually decrease the stitch length until you are barely moving, to secure the threads.

TIP Stitch with your hands positioned on either side of the walking foot, holding the fabric taut.

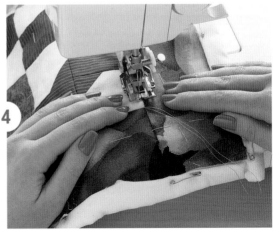

Machine-quilting Patterns

Stitch-in-the-ditch quilting emphasizes the pieced design because it is stitched following the seamlines for the blocks. Stitch so that the needle enters the well of the seam.

Channel quilting is stitched in relatively evenly spaced lines. You can mark them before you layer and baste the quilt or, for a less formal look, you can stitch them more irregularly. The quilting lines can be diagonal, vertical, or horizontal.

Outline quilting. Stitch about ¼" (6 mm) away from the seamlines.

TIP Whenever you need to change direction, stop with the needle down in the fabric. Raise the walking foot, and PIVOT. Then lower the walking foot and continue stitching.

Binding

Binding is the final step for most of your quilting projects. Enclosing the edges of the quilt, the binding forms a clean, attractive finish. Binding fabrics can either match or complement the other fabrics in the quilt. Very often a quilt is bound in the same fabric as the outer border.

Binding a Quilt

1 Cut 3" (7.5 cm) binding strips from the entire crosswise width of the fabric. If the sides of your quilt are shorter than the length of the binding strips, go on to step 3. If the sides of your quilt are longer than one binding strip, pin two strips, right sides together, at right angles. Mark a diagonal line from the corner of the upper strip to the corner of the lower strip. Stitch on the marked line.

2 Trim the seam allowances to ¼" (6 mm). Press the seam open.

3 Press the binding strips in half lengthwise, wrong sides together.

4 *Measure the quilt top across the middle*, from side to side. Cut two binding strips equal to this measurement plus 2" (5 cm). Mark the binding strips 1" (2.5 cm) from the ends. Divide the length between the pins in fourths, and pin-mark. Also divide the upper and lower edges of the quilt in fourths, and pin-mark.

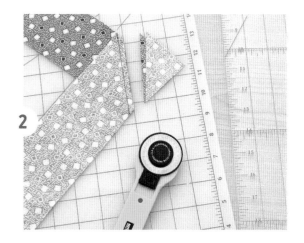

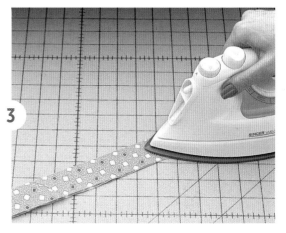

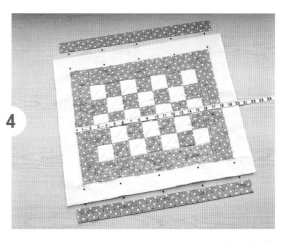

QUICK REFERENCE

Measure the quilt top across the middle. After piecing and quilting a quilt top, it is likely that the top and bottom may be slightly different lengths. By making both bindings the same length as the middle of the quilt, you are able to square up the finished project.

(continued)

Binding a Quilt continued

5 Pin a binding strip on the right side of the upper edge of the quilt, aligning the raw edges of the binding to the raw edge of the quilt top and matching the pin marks. **Insert the pins perpendicular to the raw edges**. The binding will extend 1" (2.5 cm) beyond the quilt at each end.

6 Stitch the binding strip to the quilt ¼" (6 mm) from the raw edges of the binding. **Remove the pins as you come to them**.

7 Trim off the excess batting and backing ½" (1.3 cm) from the stitching line.

8 Wrap the binding snugly around the edge of the quilt, covering the stitching line on the back of the quilt. Pin the binding in place from the right side, inserting the pins parallel to the binding in the seam "ditch" and catching the folded edge on the back. For easy removal, insert all the pins so that the heads will be toward you when you are stitching.

QUICK REFERENCE

Insert the pins perpendicular to the raw edges. This makes it easier to remove them as you sew. The pin heads are near the raw edge where you can grasp them with your right hand. In this position, you are much less likely to stick yourself with a pin as you sew.

Remove pins as you come to them. As tempting as it may be, don't sew over pins! You may be lucky and save a few seconds, or you could hit a pin and break your needle, costing you much more time in the long run.

9 Stitch in the ditch (page 43) on the right side of the quilt, catching the binding on the back of the quilt. Remove the pins as you come to them.

10 Repeat steps 5 to 9 for the lower edge of the quilt. Trim the ends of the upper and lower binding strips even with the edges of the quilt top.

11 Repeat steps 4 to 7 for the sides of the quilt, measuring the quilt top down the middle, from top to bottom, in step 4. Trim the ends of the binding strips to extend ½" (1.3 cm) beyond the finished edges of the quilt.

12 Wrap and pin the binding around the edge, as in step 8. At each end, fold in the raw edges of the binding. Then fold under the ½" (1.3 cm) end; press. Finish wrapping and pinning the binding. Stitch the binding as in step 9.

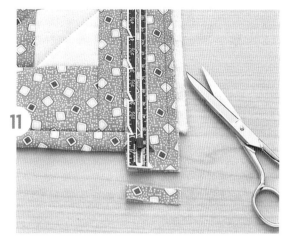

Quilting Projects

The sixteen projects in this section are loosely arranged in order of difficulty, and different quilting techniques are taught in each project. Not all quilts are flat and used for warmth or display. Some quilted items are home décor pieces or accessories that include a zipper and lining, so you will even learn a few extra sewing techniques as you quilt. While you probably will not make all the projects in order, it is well worth your time to at least read through all the projects and study the techniques introduced in each one.

Raw-edge Appliqué Hot Pad

Raw-edge appliqués add dimension and interest to a quilted project. Practice the technique by creating this maple leaf hot pad. Because the batting is quite thin, these hot pads are more decorative than useful. The edges of the leaf can be frayed with a stiff brush. For minimal fraying, use a tightly woven fabric for the appliqué. If you would like a more natural frayed look, machine wash and tumble dry the hot pad. The finished hot pad is about 9" (23 cm) square.

WHAT YOU'LL LEARN . . . .

- How to sew a raw-edge appliqué
- How to channel-quilt

WHAT YOU'LL NEED . . . .

- ⅜ yd. (0.35 m) background fabric, for the hot pad
- ¼ yd. (0.25 m) contrasting fabric, for the appliqué and binding
- Low-loft batting, about 13" (33 cm) square
- Rotary cutter and mat
- Quilting ruler
- Thread to match or blend with the fabrics
- Glue stick
- Decorative ring

How to Sew a Raw-edge Appliqué Hot Pad

1 Straighten the cut ends of the fabric, and trim off the selvages (page 33). Cut a 9" (23 cm) square of background fabric for the hot pad front. Cut a 13" (33 cm) square of background fabric for the back. Cut a 13" (33 cm) square of batting. Cut four 3" × 11" (7.5 × 28 cm) strips of contrasting fabric for the binding. **Cut a leaf appliqué (p. 53)** from the contrasting fabric, about 6" (15 cm) wide.

(continued)

2 **Glue-baste** the leaf appliqué, right side up, to the right side of the hot pad front. Position the leaf as desired in the center of the square.

3 Layer and baste the hot pad (page 36). Remove the layers from the work surface. Attach a walking foot (page 11), if you have one. Set your stitch length at 12 stitches per inch, which equals 2.5 mm. Begin stitching in the upper right corner of the pad, about 1" (2.5 cm) from the cut edge of the top layer.

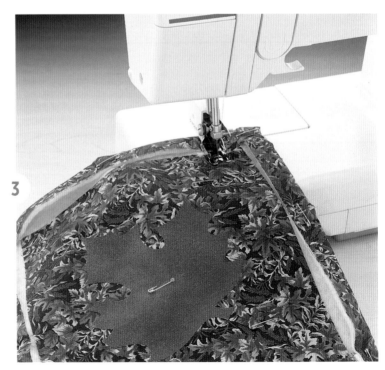

4 Stitch from top to bottom, *stopping with the needle down in the fabric*. Lift the presser foot, pivot the hot pad 90°, and lower the presser foot. Stitch about 1" (2.5 cm). Stopping with the needle down, lift the presser foot, and pivot the hot pad another 90° to begin a new row of stitching.

(continued)

QUICK REFERENCE

Cut a leaf appliqué. Draw a pattern freehand, or trace around a real leaf. Because the edges will not be finished in any way, avoid any long narrow extensions or small details that could ravel away entirely.

Glue-baste. Using a glue stick, apply dots of glue to the wrong side of the appliqué. This will hold it temporarily in place until you catch it permanently to the hot pad with quilting stitches.

Stopping with the needle down in the fabric. Stop running the machine with the foot pedal. Turn the handwheel on your machine manually until the needle is all the way down into the fabric.

How to Sew a Raw-edge Appliqué Hot Pad continued

5 Repeat this process until the entire hot pad is channel-quilted (page 43), catching the appliqué in the stitching. If you basted the hot pad with safety pins, remove them as you come to them.

6 Bind the edges of the hot pad, following the directions on page 44. Hand-stitch a small decorative ring to one corner, for hanging, if desired.

TIP Relax! The rows of channel quilting don't need to be perfectly parallel. In fact, some variation is desirable to give it handmade charm.

5

6

Variations on the Theme

Make hot pads for all seasons. Stitch a fir tree appliqué over a snowy print fabric for a winter hot pad. Get in the Halloween spirit with fall colors and a pumpkin appliqué. Or how about a spring fever hot pad?

Hand-appliquéd Zippered Bag

Quilted, zippered bags can be used to hold cosmetics, jewelry, or delicate lingerie. The simple motif appliqués are stitched invisibly to the outer fabric by hand. After construction, hand-quilted stitches are added around each design element to accent the bag's padded look. This project introduces you to the world of hand-stitched appliqués, with some neat tricks and techniques that will help you tackle other appliquéd quilts. Appliquéing and quilting by hand means you can take your project with you, and this project is small enough to make transporting it really easy.

WHAT YOU'LL LEARN..............

- How to create neat, folded-under edges around appliqué motifs
- How to hand-stitch appliqués invisibly
- How to quilt by hand
- How to sew in a zipper

WHAT YOU'LL NEED...............

- ¼ yd. (0.25 m) each of outer fabric, lining, and low-loft batting
- Scraps of fabrics for appliqués
- Rotary cutter and mat
- Quilting ruler
- Appliqué pattern
- (page 170)
- Stiff tag board or lightweight cardboard
- Spray starch
- 9" (23 cm) polyester zipper
- Sharp or between hand needle (page 22)
- Thread to match appliqué fabrics

How to Sew a Hand-appliquéd Zippered Bag

1 Straighten the cut edges of your fabrics and trim off the selvages (page 33). Cut one 8½" × 16" (21.8 × 40.5 cm) rectangle from the outer fabric, one from the batting, and one from the lining. Refer back to page 35 for cutting a rectangle wider than the ruler.

(continued)

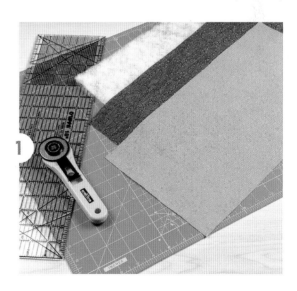

How to Sew a Hand-appliquéd Zippered Bag continued

2 Trace the appliqué patterns (page 170) onto tracing paper; cut them out. Cut out cardboard templates to the finished size of the appliqués. Place the fabric, wrong side up, on a cutting board. Adding ¼" (6 mm) fold-under allowances all around, cut around the templates, using a rotary cutter (page 32). **Clip inside curves and corners** almost up to the template; trim outside corners to within ⅛" (3 mm) of the template.

3 Place the appliqués, wrong side up, on a pressing surface; center the templates over them. Spray starch into a small bowl. Using your finger, dab a little starch along the fold-under allowance. With the tip of a dry iron, press the allowance over the edge of the template; press until the starch dries. Continue pressing around the appliqué, encasing the template. Remove the templates. Turn the appliqués over and press from the right side.

4 Place the apple appliqué on one end of the outer fabric, so the center of the apple is 4½" (11.5 cm) from the end. Pin in place, using two small safety pins. Pin the leaf appliqué in place.

5 Thread a between needle (page 22) with a single strand of red thread. ***Tie a knot in the end.*** Insert the needle from the back of the fabric, coming up just under the folded edge of the apple appliqué. Catch only a tiny bit of the fold. Pull the needle and thread completely through to the front; the knot will catch on the underside. Reinsert the tip of the needle into the background fabric directly beneath the exit point on the appliqué fold. Run the needle tip under the background fabric about ⅛" (3 mm), coming back through to the front just under the folded edge of the appliqué, again catching a tiny bit of the fold. Pull the needle and thread completely through to the front and ***pull the stitches snug***.

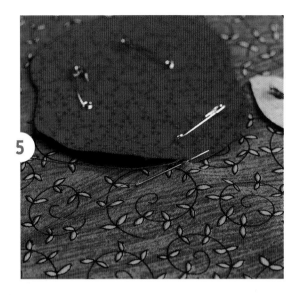

6 Continue stitching around the appliqué, taking tiny ⅛" (3 mm) stitches, until you are back to the starting point. Draw the thread to the underside. Next to the exit point, take a tiny stitch through the background fabric under the appliqué. Just before the thread loop disappears, run the needle through it and pull snug. Repeat once more and cut the thread.

(continued)

QUICK REFERENCE

Clip inside curves and corners. This will allow the fabric to spread and fit the curve or corner when the edge is pressed under.

Tie a knot in the end. Lay the tail end of the thread on the needle and hold it in place with your right thumb. Then wrap the thread around the needle, toward the point, three times. Close your left thumb and index finger over the wrappings and tail. Slide them down over the eye of the needle and down the entire length of the thread to the end. A small knot will form.

Pull the stitches snug. After every two or three stitches, pull the thread snug so that the appliqué hugs the background fabric tightly, but not so tightly that it puckers. Your stitches should pretty much disappear.

TIP If at any time the thread grows too short, end the stitching as in step 6 and begin again with a new length of thread as in step 5.

How to Sew a Hand-appliquéd Zippered Bag continued

7 Repeat steps 5 and 6 for the leaf appliqué, using green thread. Spray the batting with a light layer of temporary fabric adhesive. Smooth the outer rectangle, right side up, over the batting.

TIP Lay the batting in the bottom of a large box. The sides and bottom of the box will catch any over-spray of adhesive, protecting your workspace.

8 Pin the closed zipper to one upper edge of the outer fabric, right sides together, aligning the edge of the zipper tape to the raw edge of the fabric. The ends of the zipper should extend beyond the fabric edges. Attach a zipper foot to your sewing machine. Stitch the zipper in place, ¼" (6 mm) from the edge.

9 Align the other side of the zipper to the opposite end of the bag, right sides together. Fold the stitched edge out of the way. Stitch the remaining side of the zipper in place.

10 Open the zipper. Place the lining and the outer bag right sides together, aligning the upper edges on one end, and sandwiching the zipper between them. With the fleece facing up, stitch over the previous stitches. Repeat at the opposite end.

11 Close the zipper partway so the tab is near the center of the top. Pin the side seams, right sides together, with lining to lining and outer fabric to outer fabric. **Insert the pins perpendicular to the edges (p. 46)**. Match the zipper seamlines, and turn the zipper teeth toward the outer bag. Attach a general purpose presser foot. Stitch ¼" (6 mm) seams, leaving a 3" (7.5 cm) opening on one side of the lining. **Remove the pins as you come to them (p. 46)**. Slow your stitching and stitch carefully, turning the handwheel by hand, as you stitch over the zipper.

12 Cut off the ends of the zipper even with the bag edges. Reach in through the opening and open the zipper. Turn the bag right side out through the opening.

(continued)

10

11

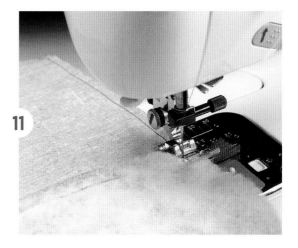

12

13 Turn in the seam allowances at the opening. Slipstitch the opening closed, alternating small stitches from one side of the opening to the other as shown.

14 Fold the bag inside the lining. Gently push the lower corners out so the bag fits smoothly. Flatten one lower corner into a triangle, with the seamline in the center. Pin. Stitch across the corner, 1½" (3.8 cm) from the point, perpendicular to the seamline. Backstitch at the beginning and end. Repeat at the other corner.

15 Turn the bag right side out. Smooth the lining into the sides and bottom of the bag. Using small safety pins, pin the layers together in several places on the front. Thread a between needle (page 22) with a single strand of thread to match the background fabric. Tie a knot in the end. Quilt by hand (page 41) around the appliqué shapes.

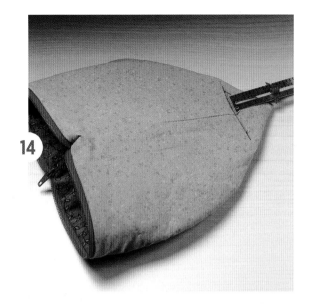

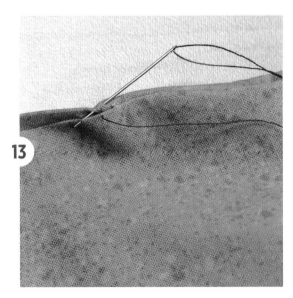

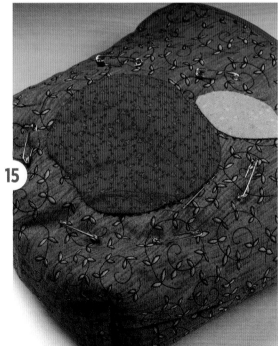

Another Style

Cut design motifs from one fabric, allowing ¼"
(6 mm) allowances around them. Then appliqué
them to the surface of another fabric. Accent the
appliqués with quilting stitches around the outer
edges and along inner design lines. For a ready-
made strap, hand-tack the tassels of a chair tie to
the sides of the bag.

Quilt-as-you-go Christmas Stocking

The technique used for this Christmas stocking is an easy way to create lively fabric arrangements with very little planning or precutting. The batting is layered over the backing fabric, and the quilt pieces are sewn together through the layers, essentially piecing and quilting all at once. Strips of various fabrics are stitched at different angles to create a slightly haphazard appearance. You determine the shape of each piece as you stitch it on. Select four to six different fabrics, some plain colors and some printed, in a variety of scales and colors.

How to Sew a Quilt-as-you-go Christmas Stocking

1 Enlarge the pattern on page 171, and cut it out. Fold the backing fabric in half lengthwise, matching the selvages. Place the pattern on the fabric near the selvages, with the grainline arrow going in the same direction as the selvages. Be sure to allow room for the cuff near the fabric fold. Pin the pattern to the fabric at one end of the **grainline arrow (p. 66)**. Measure from the arrow to the selvage. Then measure from the opposite end of the arrow to the selvage, and adjust the pattern **so the measurements are the same (p. 66);** pin in place through both layers of fabric. Pin the pattern to the fabric all around the outer edge, inserting pins about every 3" (7.5 cm). Cut out the backing.

(continued)

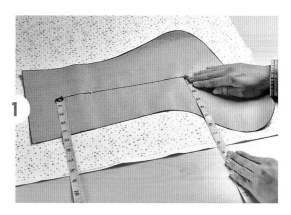

How to Sew a Quilt-as-you-go Christmas Stocking *continued*

2 Along the fabric fold, cut out a 16½" × 4" (42 × 10 cm) rectangle for the cuff; with the double layer, the full width will be 8" (20.5 cm). Cut a 16½" × 4" rectangle of batting for the cuff. Cut each of the piecing fabrics into 3" (7.5 cm) strips on the crosswise grain.

3 Cut two stocking pieces from the batting. Place the backing pieces wrong side up. Spray lightly with temporary fabric adhesive. Smooth a batting piece over each backing piece, aligning the outer edges.

4 Plan out the sequence and general size and angle of the piecing strips. Place the strip that goes across the ankle to the heal, right side up, over the batting. Pin in place down the center. Trim off the strip end just beyond the stocking edge.

QUICK REFERENCE

Grainline arrow. All of the pieces in any commercial pattern have an arrow on them that indicates which direction the pattern should be placed on the fabric. Aligning this arrow to the lengthwise grain of the fabric provides the most stability, the best fit, or the most flattering drape.

So the measurements are the same. When the arrow is parallel to the selvages, the pattern piece will be positioned properly on the grainline. Though proper grainline positioning is not crucial to the success of your stocking, this is a good lesson to learn for any sewing project that involves a commercial pattern.

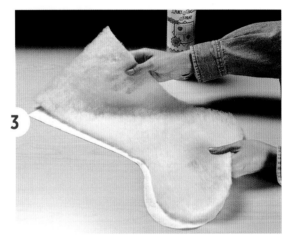

5 Working toward the toe, pin the next strip over the first, right sides together, at a slightly skewed angle. Using a straight stitch of about 12 stitches per inch or 4 mm, stitch through all layers, stitching ¼" (6 mm) from the cut edge of the top strip.

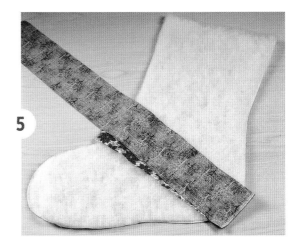

6 Turn the second strip right side up, and finger-press along the seamline. Trim off the strip end just beyond the stocking edges.

7 Repeat steps 5 and 6 with various fabric strips until the foot and toe are completely covered. Change the angle and width of each strip to achieve a haphazard appearance. Then work off the opposite side of the first strip to the upper edge of the stocking.

(continued)

How to Sew a Quilt-as-you-go Christmas Stocking *continued*

8 Pin the top and toe pieces in place along the outer edges. Place the pieced stocking front, backing side up, under the presser foot, and stitch *a scant ¼" (6 mm) from the edge* of the backing. Trim the edges of the pieced fabric and batting even with the backing. Set the front aside.

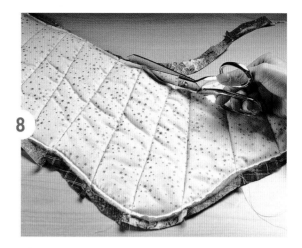

9 Repeat steps 4 to 8 for the stocking back. Pin the stocking front and back, right sides together, inserting the pins perpendicular to the edges. Stitch *¼" (6 mm) from the edges* around the stocking, leaving the upper edge open.

QUICK REFERENCE

A scant ¼" (6 mm) from the edge. Placing this stitching line between the actual ¼" (6 mm) stitching line and the raw edge prevents it from showing when the stocking front and back are sewn together and turned right sides out.

¼" (6 mm) from the edges. In a previous step, you stitched a scant ¼" (6 mm) from the edges. Stitch just to the left of that first stitching line now, so your first stitching line won't show on the outside of the stocking.

Press a crease. Your cuff may already have a crease. If your fabric came from the store folded in half with the right sides together, press out the crease. Then refold it with the wrong sides together, and press a new crease.

Fabric marker. Use one of the quilt marking tools described on page 21 or a water-erasable fabric marking pen as shown here. Test the water-erasable marker first on a scrap of cuff fabric to be sure the marks will disappear completely when dabbed with a wet cloth.

10 Fold the cuff in half lengthwise, wrong sides together, and **press a crease**. Then fold it in half crosswise, but don't press it. With the long open edges at the top and the short open ends at the side where you want the hanger to be, plan the placement of the name. Lightly write the name, using a **fabric marker**.

11 Open out the cuff. Spray one side of the cuff batting lightly with temporary fabric adhesive. Smooth it into place on the wrong side of the cuff, aligning it to the outer edges on one half of the cuff. Fold the cuff in half crosswise, right sides together, forming a circle; stitch the short ends together with a ¼" (6 mm) seam. Finger-press the seam allowances open. Then fold the cuff in half, wrong sides together, and stitch the upper edges together ¼" (6 mm) from the edges.

12 Hand-quilt the name, following the general directions on page 41. Use double strand of thread in a color to coordinate with the stocking. Remove any marked lines that still show.

(continued)

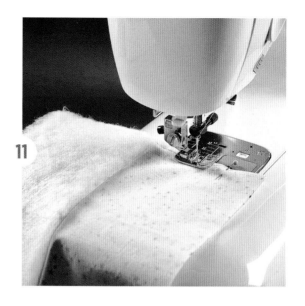

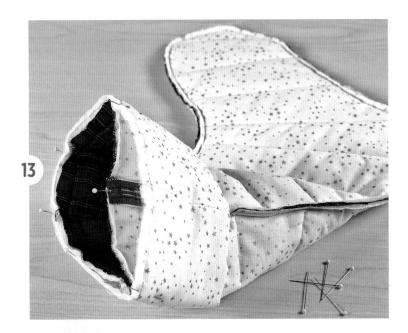

13 Fold the ribbon hanger in half, and pin it over the stocking back seamline, aligning the cut ends to the stocking top. Pin the cuff to the stocking top, aligning the cut edges and seamlines, with the right side of the cuff against t he stocking backing. Stitch ¼" (6 mm) seam.

14 Turn the stocking right side out; turn the cuff out and down. Put your hand inside and push the stocking seamline out to the edge with your fingers.

Another Style

Create a rustic Christmas stocking (opposite) using cotton flannels. Tear the fabrics into 3" (7.5 cm) strips on the cross-wise grain, and remove one or two fraying yarns from the torn edges. Begin at the toe and work upward, layering each strip, right side up, over the previous one and stitching ¼" (6 mm) from the torn edge.

Paper-pieced Holiday Coasters

This festive coaster set introduces you to the popular quilting technique of paper piecing or foundation piecing. Fabric pieces are roughly cut for each numbered section of a paper pattern. Translucent foundation paper, available at quilt shops, works very well because you can see through it without having to hold it to a light source. With fabrics aligned on the underside of the pattern, the pieces are stitched together through the lines on the paper, one piece at a time in a numbered sequence. Seam allowances are trimmed down after each stitching line, eliminating the need for precise cutting of the design pieces beforehand. Each design goes together in minutes, and it's nearly impossible to make a mistake!

WHAT YOU'LL LEARN...............

- The basic techniques of paper piecing
- How to finger-press seam allowances
- How to line to the edge
- How to slipstitch

WHAT YOU'LL NEED...............

- Translucent foundation paper
- Patterns (pages 172 to 175)
- #2 pencil or fine-point permanent marker
- Small straightedge
- Small scraps of various fabrics in small-grain prints and solid colors, as suggested in the photo
- ¼ yd. (0.25 m) extra-low-loft batting
- ¼ yd. (0.25 m) fabric for borders and lining
- Temporary fabric adhesive
- Hand needle and thread

How to Sew a Paper-pieced Coaster

1 Trace the patterns on pages 172 to 175 onto foundation paper, using a fine-point permanent marker or #2 pencil. Cut out the patterns, allowing a ½" (1.3 cm) margin around the outside. Number the design sections. The side with the lines is actually the pattern back. The fabrics will be sewn to the blank or front side. Cut a piece of fabric for each section of the design, making each piece about ¾" (2 cm) larger than the area it has to cover. The pieces can be square, rectangular, or irregular.

(continued)

How to Sew a Paper-pieced Coaster continued

2 Place the pattern so the blank (right) side faces up. Center and pin the first fabric piece over section 1, with the right side of the fabric facing up. Pin in place, *inserting the pin where it won't interfere with stitching lines*. Check from the back (printed side) to see that the fabric extends at least ¼" (6 mm) beyond all the lines for section 1.

3 Place the second fabric piece over the first piece, right sides together, roughly aligning the raw edges between sections 1 and 2. Pin along the shared pattern line, with the pin inserted on the line.

4 Flip the second fabric piece over to confirm that the fabric extends at least ¼" (6 mm) beyond the section 2 lines. Adjust the position of the second piece, if necessary. Fold the second piece back, right sides together, over the first. Move the pin to a place away from the stitching line.

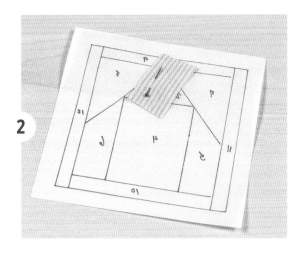

2

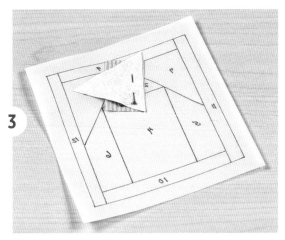

3

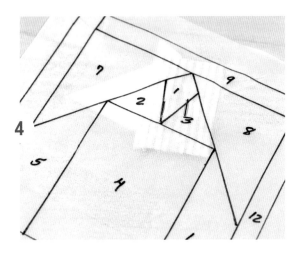

4

QUICK REFERENCE

Inserting the pin where it won't interfere with stitching lines. The pin will be on the underside as you stitch, and difficult to move out of the way. Place it where it won't be run over by the presser foot or hit by the needle. With some practice, you will be able to paper-piece without using pins at all.

Short straight stitch. Stitches that are closer together will be more difficult to remove if you make a mistake, but they are also more secure and make it easier to tear away the paper after the design is sewn.

Trim the seam allowances ¼" (6 mm) beyond the stitching line. Fold the paper out of the way and trim off the excess fabric to within ¼" (6 mm) of the stitching line, using a scissors. The seam allowances do not have to be accurately cut.

5 Set the machine for a **short straight stitch** of 12 to 15 stitches per inch or 2 mm. Place the pattern, printed side up, under the presser foot, with the needle aligned to the shared stitching line between sections 1 and 2. Lower the presser foot and begin stitching two or three stitch lengths before the line. Stitch on the line to the end and stitch two or three stitches beyond the end of the line. Raise the presser foot. Carefully remove the pattern and fabric from the machine, clipping the threads close to the pattern.

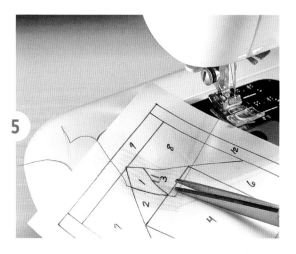

6 Remove the pins. Flip the pattern over and **trim the seam allowances down to about ¼" (6 mm) beyond the stitching line**. Finger-press the second fabric away from the first along the stitching line.

TIP Finger-pressing saves time. Rather than running over to the ironing board after the addition of each piece, the fabrics are temporarily smoothed into place with your fingers. Place the pattern right side up on a flat surface. Flip the just-sewn piece over so the right side faces out. Run your fingernail over the seam to flatten it and extend the piece to its full size.

(continued)

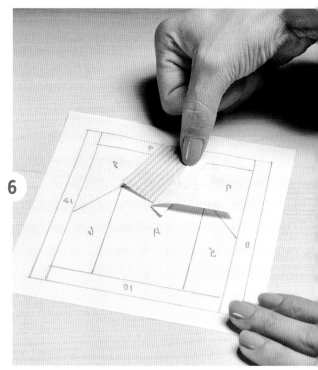

How to Sew a Paper-pieced Coaster *continued*

7 Place the third fabric piece over the second piece, right sides together. Pin along the shared pattern line, with the pin inserted on the line. Flip the third piece over to confirm that the fabric extends at least ¼" (6 mm) beyond the section 3 lines. Adjust the position of the third piece, if necessary. Fold the third piece back over the second. Repin the fabric in place away from the stitching line.

8 Stitch on the shared design line between sections 2 and 3, as in step 6. Trim the seam allowances and finger-press the third piece as in steps 7 and 8. Follow the same procedure, adding pieces in numbered sequence until the entire pattern is complete.

9 Stitch around the entire pattern, just outside the outer design line. Press. Trim off the excess fabric ¼" (6 mm) beyond the stitching line. Carefully tear away the paper from the back of the design.

8

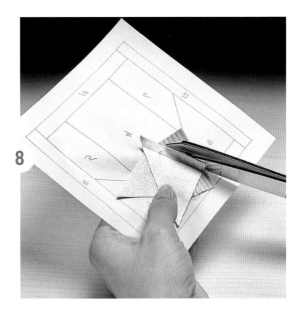

7

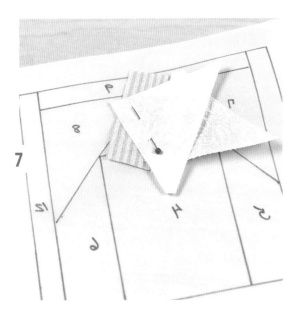

9

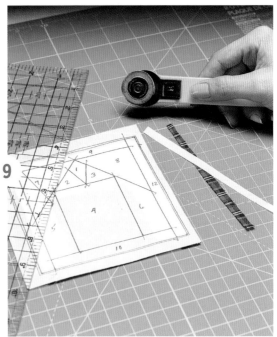

10 Cut a 5" (12.7 cm) square for the backing and a 5" (12.7 cm) square of the batting. Spray a light coat of temporary fabric adhesive to one side of the batting. Smooth the pieced coaster, right side up, over the batting. Place backing over the pieced top, right sides together. Pin the layers together, **inserting the pins perpendicular to the edges (p. 46)**. Stitch ¼" (6 mm) seam all around, pivoting at the corners. Leave a 2" (5 cm) opening along the bottom edge for turning.

11 Trim the batting close to the stitching. Trim the corners diagonally to reduce bulk.

12 Turn the coaster right side out through the opening; press. Using a hand needle and thread, slipstitch the opening closed, alternating small stitches from one side of the opening to the other as shown.

13 Attach a walking foot (page 11) and lengthen the stitch length slightly. Quilt the coaster by stitching in the ditch of the seam (page 43) between the outer border and the design.

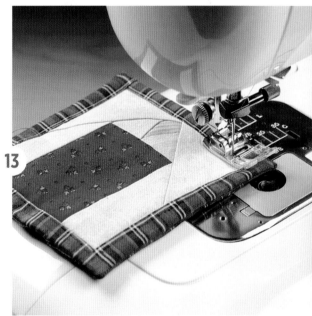

Variations for Paper-pieced Designs

Make a Christmas wall hanging from your designs. After piecing the fronts, join them into a strip, using ¼" (6 mm) seam allowances. Cut the backing and batting to the same size as the strip. Complete the hanging by stitching in the ditch around the border and between the blocks. Add a ribbon hanger. Accent the designs with ribbon, beads, or sequins as desired.

Turn your designs into Christmas ornaments, simply by adding hangers. Braid three lengths of embroidery floss together and knot the ends. Then hand-stitch the knots to the upper corners of the ornaments.

Nine-patch Pillow

This charming pillow for your bedroom or living room is made by stitching nine squares of fabric together in a checkerboard pattern. You'll need to select two coordinating prints, a coordinating print and solid, or two contrasting solids. The checkerboard pattern is repeated on the back side of the pillow, with the squares arranged in the reverse order.

WHAT YOU'LL LEARN.............

- The importance of accuracy in both cutting and stitching
- Tricks for perfectly matched seams
- How to stitch in the ditch

WHAT YOU'LL NEED..............

- ½ yd. (0.5 m) each of two coordinating fabrics
- ⅝ yd. (0.6 m) muslin, for the pillow backing
- ⅝ yd. (0.6 m) batting
- Rotary cutter and mat
- Quilting ruler
- Thread to match or blend with the fabrics
- 18" (46 cm) square pillow form
- Hand needle

How to Sew a Nine-patch Pillow

1 Straighten the cut ends of the fabrics, and trim off the selvages (page 33). With the fabric still folded in half, cut two 6½" (16.5 cm) strips of fabric across the entire width, from the cut edges to the fold.

2 Cut nine 6½" (16.5 cm) squares from these strips.

(continued)

How to Sew a Nine-patch Pillow *continued*

3 Repeat steps 1 and 2 for fabric B. Arrange the squares in two nine-patch blocks, as shown.

4 Pin one A square to one B square along one side, with right sides together, ***inserting pins perpendicular to the edges (p. 46)***. Align the cut ends and edges. Place the fabric under the presser foot, aligning the upper edges to the needle hole in the throat plate. Align the cut edges of the fabric to the ¼" (6 mm) seam allowance guide (page 18) on your machine. Stitch a ¼" (6 mm) seam, ***removing pins as you come to them (p. 46)***.

5 Pin another A square to the opposite side of the B square. Stitch a ¼" (6 mm) seam, forming a three-square strip.

6 Repeat steps 4 and 5 to make two more identical three-square strips. Then sew the remaining strips together, with an A square in the center of each. Press the seam allowances **toward the darker fabric**. The strips should now measure 6½" × 18½" (16.5 × 47 cm).

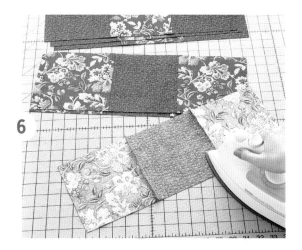

7 Beginning with the pillow front, pin the top strip to the center strip, with right sides together and raw edges even. Align the seams, **inserting the pins in the wells of the seams**. You will notice that the matching seam allowances turn in opposite directions. Stitch a ¼" (6 mm) seam, removing pins as you come to them.

TIP To ensure smooth seams and perfect intersections, slow down as you approach each one. Stop with the needle down in the fabric, raise the presser foot, and lift the strips slightly from the machine bed. Make sure the seam allowances on the underside are still turned in the direction they were pressed. Then lower the presser foot and continue sewing.

8 Pin the remaining strip to the opposite side of the center strip, pinning as in step 7; stitch the seam. You have just completed a nine-patch block. Press both seam allowances away from the center.

(continued)

QUICK REFERENCE

Toward the darker fabric. In piecing a quilt top, seam allowances are often pressed toward darker pieces to avoid show-through under light-colored pieces.

Inserting the pins in the wells of the seams. By pinning in this manner, you are making sure that the stitched seams will line up perfectly on the right side. Stitch up to these pins as close as you can before removing them.

How to Sew a Nine-patch Pillow continued

9 Repeat steps 7 and 8 for the pillow back. Cut two squares of muslin and two squares of batting, each 4" (10 cm) larger than the pillow front and back. Layer and baste the front and back (page 36).

10 Remove the layers from the work surface. Set your stitch length at 10 to 12 stitches per inch, which equals 2.5 mm. Attach a walking foot (page 11), if you have one, or use an all-purpose presser foot. Quilt each block, using the stitch-in-the-ditch method (page 43) along all the seams.

11 Set your stitch length to long, and machine-baste around the pillow top *a scant ¼"* *(6 mm) from the edge (p. 69)* of the top fabric. Trim the batting and muslin even with the edges of the top fabric, using a rotary cutter and mat. Repeat for the pillow back.

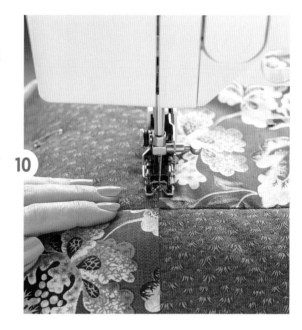

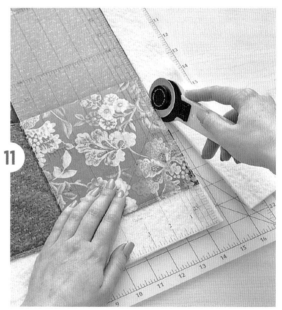

12 Place the pillow back over the pillow front, with right sides together, matching the raw edges. Align the seams of the front block to the corresponding seams of the back block. Insert pins in the wells of the seams.

13 Stitch around the pillow cover, ¼" (6 mm) from the raw edges (p.69), leaving a 10" (25.5 cm) opening along one side. Trim the corners diagonally, to remove excess bulk.

14 Turn the pillow cover right side out through the opening. Use a point turner or similar tool to carefully push the corners out, if necessary. Insert the pillow form into the pillow cover. Pin the opening closed. Slipstitch the opening closed, alternating small stitches from one side of the opening to the other as shown.

Checkerboard Placemats

Add homespun charm to your dining table with this set of four checkerboard placemats. Select two coordinating print fabrics, a print and a solid, or two solids, preferably with a high contrast between them. Then make quick-and-easy napkins to match.

The directions are for four placemats. You will find that this strip-piecing method of construction saves time in sewing and cuts down on the number of trips back and forth to the ironing board. Set your machine for a straight stitch of 10 to 12 stitches per inch, which equals 2.5 mm, and sew ¼" (6 mm) seam allowances throughout the entire project. Each placemat measures about 14" × 18" (35.5 × 46 cm).

WHAT YOU'LL LEARN..............

- Strip piecing saves time
- How to add a border to your quilt project
- How to sew double-fold hems on napkins

WHAT YOU'LL NEED...............

- ½ yd. (0.5 m) light-colored print or solid fabric, we'll call "A"
- 2 yd. (1.85 m) darker-colored print or solid fabric, we'll call "B"
- Additional fabric, for napkins (A or B)
- Low-loft polyester or poly/cotton blend batting
- Rotary cutter and mat
- Quilting ruler
- Thread to match fabric A

How to Sew Checkerboard Placemats

1 Straighten the cut ends of the fabrics, and trim off the selvages (page 33). Cut five 2½" (6.5 cm) strips from the entire crosswise width of fabric A. Cut five 2½" (6.5 cm) strips from the entire crosswise width of fabric B.

(continued)

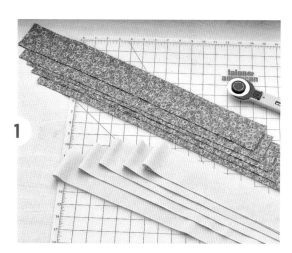

2 Cut seven 2½" (6.5 cm) strips from the entire crosswise width of fabric B, for the border. Cut seven 3" (7.5 cm) strips from the entire crosswise width of fabric B, for the binding.

3 Pin an A strip and a B strip right sides together, aligning the long edges; **insert the pins perpendicular to the long edge (p. 46)**. Stitch the strips together, **removing the pins as you come to them (p. 46)**. Then stitch another A strip to the other side of the B strip, in the same manner. Continue adding strips, alternating fabrics, until you have three A strips and two B strips. Press the seam allowances **toward the darker fabric (p. 83)** (B).

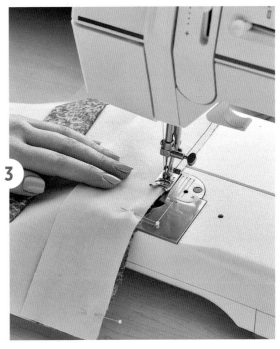

4 Stitch three B strips and two A strips together, as in step 3, with fabrics alternating in the opposite sequence. Press the seam allowances toward the darker fabric (B).

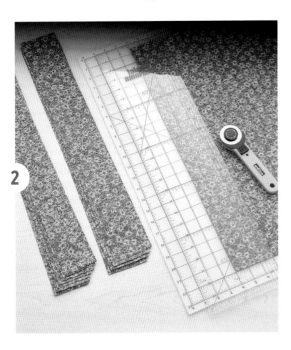

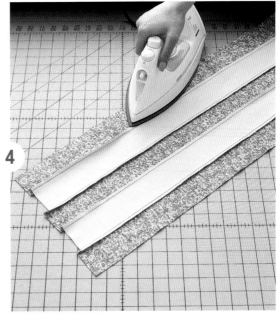

5 Cut the pieced strip sets, perpendicular to the seams, into 2½" (6.5 cm) strips.

TIP If your fabric is 45" (115 cm) wide, you should be able to cut at least seventeen small strips from each set. You will need sixteen of one set and twelve of the other to complete four placemats.

6 Align the raw edges of two different strips, right sides together, matching the seams. The seam allowances will be pressed in opposite directions. **Insert a pin in the well of the seams (p. 83)**, to make sure they line up exactly. Stitch the strips together, removing the pins as you come to them and keeping the seam allowances turned in opposite directions.

7 Add five more strips as in step 6, alternating patterns, for a total of seven strips. Press all the new seam allowances in the same direction.

(continued)

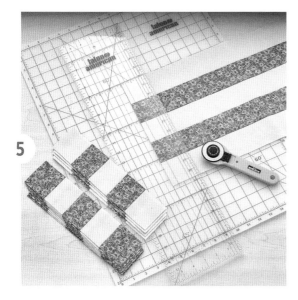

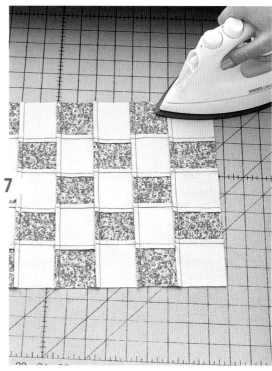

8 ***Measure the placemat lengthwise across the middle (p. 45).*** Cut two border strips equal to this measurement. Pin one strip to the top of the placemat; pin the other strip to the bottom. Align the ends of the strips to the sides of the placemat. Stretch the strips or the placemat slightly, if necessary, to make them fit. Stitch ¼" (6 mm) seams; press the seam allowances toward the borders.

9 Measure the placemat widthwise across the center, including the new borders. Cut two border strips equal to this measurement. Pin a strip to each side of the placemat, aligning the ends of the strips to the top and bottom edges of the placemat. Stretch the strips or the placemat slightly, if necessary, to make them fit. Stitch ¼" (6 mm) seams; press the seam allowances toward the borders.

10 Repeat steps 6 to 9 for the three other placemats. Cut the backing fabric and batting 4" (10 cm) longer and wider than the placemat. Layer and baste the placemats (page 36).

11 Attach a walking foot (page 11). Quilt by stitching in the ditch (page 43), **following this sequence**: Begin with a vertical seam near the center, then a horizontal seam near the center. Then stitch in the ditch of the seam between the border and pieced section. Finish by stitching the remaining vertical seams between rows and the remaining horizontal seams between rows. Bind each placemat, following the directions on page 44.

QUICK REFERENCE

Following this sequence. By quilting in this sequence, you first anchor the quilt vertically and horizontally, preventing the layers from shifting.

How to Sew Napkins

1 Cut squares for the napkins 1" (2.5 cm) larger than the desired finished size. Press under ½" (1.3 cm) on each side of the napkin. Unfold the corner, and refold it diagonally so that the pressed folds match. Press the diagonal fold, and trim the corner as shown. Repeat for each corner.

TIP For the most efficient use of your fabric, cut three 15" (38 cm) squares from 45" (115 cm) fabric or 18" (46 cm) squares from 54" (137 cm) fabric.

2 Fold the raw edges under to meet the pressed fold, forming a double-fold hem The corners will form neat diagonal folds. Press the folds; pin only if necessary.

3 Stitch the hem close to the inner fold, using a short straight stitch and beginning along one side. At the corners, stop with the needle down in the fabric, between the diagonal folds, and pivot. Overlap the stitches about ½" (1.3 cm) where they meet.

More Placemat Ideas

Quilt the checkerboard pattern in diagonal rows. Simply follow a path from corner to corner. Try to stitch continually from edge to edge as long as possible without stopping and cutting the thread.

Paint a design in the corner of each napkin, taking inspiration from the printed fabric used in the placemat. Use fabric paints; follow the manufacturer's directions for setting the paint.

Double Nine-patch Table Topper

The double nine-patch block is a popular variation of the nine-patch block, found on page 81. This pattern alternates one-piece squares and checkerboard squares. Each of the checkerboard squares is made from nine smaller squares. The blocks are set off by sashing, another popular quilting technique.

This table topper can be made in any color scheme for holiday or everyday use. Choose a low-loft batting so the finished piece lies relatively flat on your table. All seam allowances throughout the project are ¼" (6 mm). The finished size is about 40" (102 cm) square.

WHAT YOU'LL LEARN...............

- How to add sashing to the design of your quilt
- How to quilt diagonally
- The importance of accuracy in cutting and stitching

WHAT YOU'LL NEED...............

- ⅝ yd. (0.6 m) fabric A, for small squares in the double nine-patch blocks and for the sashing squares (red)
- 2⅔ yd. (2.48 m) fabric B, for other small squares in double nine-patch blocks, for larger squares in double nine-patch, and for backing (white)
- ⅛ yd. (0.8 m) fabric C, for sashing strips and binding (blue)
- Low-loft batting, about 44" (112 cm) square
- Rotary cutter and mat
- Quilting ruler
- Thread

How to Sew a Double Nine-patch Table Topper

1 Straighten the cut ends of the fabrics, and trim off the selvages (page 33). Cut ten 1½" (3.8 cm) strips from the entire crosswise width of fabric A. Cut eight 1½" (3.8 cm) strips from the entire crosswise width of fabric B.

(continued)

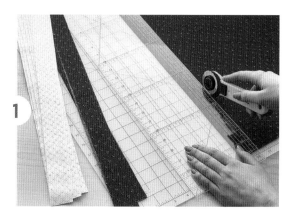

How to Sew a Double Nine-patch Table Topper continued

2 Pin an A strip and a B strip right sides together, aligning the long edges; **insert the pins perpendicular to the long edge (p. 46)**. Stitch the strips together, **removing the pins as you come to them (p. 46)**. Then stitch another A strip to the other side of the B strip, in the same manner.

3 Repeat step 2 until you have four sets of A-B-A strips. Then make two sets of B-A-B strips, in the same manner. Press all the seam allowances **toward the darker fabric (p. 83)** (A).

4 Cut the pieced strip sets perpendicular to the seams, into 1½" (3.8 cm) strips.

TIP If your fabric is 45" (115 cm) wide, you should be able to cut at least 28 small strips from each set. You will need 90 of one set and 45 of the other to complete the table topper.

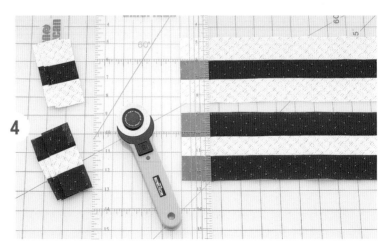

5 Align the long edge of an A-B-A strip to the long edge of a B-A-B strip, right sides together, matching the seams. The seam allowances will be pressed in opposite directions. ***Insert a pin in the well of the seams (p. 83)***, to make sure they line up exactly. Stitch the strips together, removing the pins as you come to them and keeping the seam allowances turned in the opposite directions. Stitch another A-B-A strip to the opposite side of the B-A-B strip in the same manner.

6 Repeat step 5 until you have made 45 pieced squares. Press the seams on each square toward the outside edges.

7 Cut three 3½" (9 cm) strips from the entire crosswise width of fabric B. Then cut these strips into 3½" (9 cm) squares. You will need 36 squares in all.

(continued)

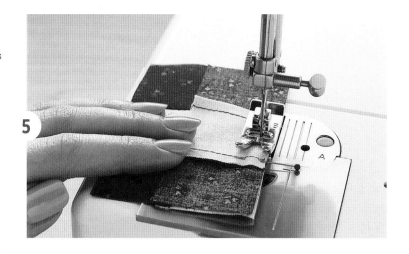

How to Sew a Double Nine-patch Table Topper continued

8 Stitch the pieced squares and the whole squares together in three-square strips. You'll need 18 strips that have pieced squares at the ends and nine strips that have whole squares at the ends. Press all the seam allowances toward the whole squares.

9 Stitch the strips for a double nine-patch block together, arranging them as shown. Take the time to insert a pin in the well of the seams, to ensure perfect seam intersections. Repeat this step until you have made nine double nine-patch blocks. Press the new seam allowances away from the center.

10 Cut six 3½" (9 cm) strips from the entire crosswise width of fabric C, for the sashing. **Measure the sides of several blocks to determine the shortest measurement.** Then cut the sashing into 24 strips with this length.

8

9

QUICK REFERENCE

Measure the sides of several blocks to determine the shortest measurement. Ideally, the blocks should measure 9½" (24 cm), but there are likely to be slight variances in seam allowance depths as you piece the blocks together. By cutting all the sashing strips to the same measurement, however, you will be able to "correct" the variances and square up the table topper.

Connecting squares. Sometimes sashing strips travel uninterrupted from one side of the quilt to the other. However, in this project, the sashing is made up of short pieces, alternating with contrasting squares. These squares "connect" pieces of the sashing in both directions, while adding an interesting design element to the overall pieced pattern of the table topper.

10

11 Cut two 3½" (9 cm) strips from the entire crosswise width of fabric A. Then cut the A strips into 3½" (9 cm) **connecting squares**; you'll need 16. Arrange the blocks, sashing strips, and connecting squares on a flat surface, as shown.

12 Stitch the first horizontal row of sashing strips and blocks together, keeping the pieces in their arranged order. Align the ends of the strips to the upper and lower edges of the blocks, easing the blocks to fit as necessary. It is easiest to stitch with the sashing strip up, keeping the seam allowances of the pieced block turned in the direction they were pressed.

TIP Use pins if you feel it would give you more control.

13 Repeat step 12 until you have pieced all three rows. Press all the seam allowances toward the sashing strips. Return the sashed block rows to the surface.

(continued)

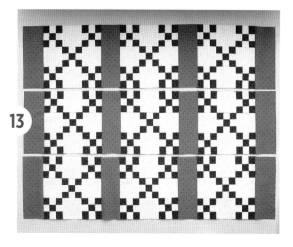

14 Stitch the horizontal rows of sashing strips and connecting squares together, keeping the pieces in their arranged order. Press all the seam allowances toward the sashing strips. Return the sashing units to the surface between the sashed block rows.

15 Place the bottom sashing unit along the lower edge of the bottom sashed block row, with right sides together, matching the seams. Insert pins in the wells of the seams, easing in any fullness. Stitch the rows together, stitching with the sashing unit facing up and removing the pins as you come to them. Take care to keep all the seam allowances turned in the direction they were pressed.

16 Continue joining the sashing units and sashed block rows, as in step 15, keeping the pieces in their arranged order, until you have completed the entire table topper. Press all the new seams toward the sashing units.

17 Place the table topper on a flat surface. With a quilting ruler and fabric marker, lightly mark diagonal quilting lines, bisecting the center of each double nine-patch block and running off the edge. Cut the backing fabric and batting 4" (10 cm) longer and wider than the table topper. Layer and baste the topper as on page 36.

TIP This marking step is much easier (and more accurate) to do now, before layering and basting, because the fabric is relatively flat and smooth. If you think you can "eyeball" the quilting lines that cut diagonally through the squares, simply mark the lines where they cross the connecting squares.

18 Attach a walking foot (page 11). Machine-quilt on the marked lines. Begin by *stitching diagonally* through the center, first in one direction and then in the other. Finish by stitching the remaining diagonal rows. Cut four 3" (7.5 cm) strips from the entire crosswise width of fabric C, for the binding. Bind the topper, following the directions on page 44.

QUICK REFERENCE

Stitching diagonally means you are stitching on the bias and the fabric has much more give. A walking foot is important here, in order to avoid puckers. Spacing your basting stitches or safety pins closer together will help, too.

Pieced Sashing Table Runner

This table runner, with pieced sashing and quilted motifs, will add a personal decorating touch to your dining room table. The motifs in the center of each square offer an opportunity to practice quilting by hand (page 41). The sashing is made of four hand-dyed fabrics with graduated color values from light to dark. These are often sold in quilt shops, already cut into pieces called Fat quarters. Select a print fabric for the large center squares and the connecting squares (p. 99) of the sashing. Then select four graduating colors that accent the print.

The finished size is approximately 52" × 16" (132 × 40.5 cm). All seam allowances for this project are ¼" (6 mm). Select machine-quilting thread in a color to match or blend with the fabrics; select hand-quilting thread (page 22) in a contrasting color.

WHAT YOU'LL LEARN..............

- How to select and use fabrics in graduated color values
- How to make pieced sashing
- How to make your own quilting template
- Hand-quilting techniques

WHAT YOU'LL NEED...............

- 2 yd. (1.85 m) printed fabric A for large blocks, connecting squares in sashing, backing, and binding
- Four hand-dyed fabrics in fat quarters, or ¼ yd. (0.25 m) each of four full-width fabrics in graduated color values, for the sashing
- Low-loft batting, about 56" × 20" (142 × 51 cm)
- Rotary cutter and mat
- Quilting ruler
- Thread for machine quilting; thread for hand quilting
- Between or sharp hand needle (page 22)
- Heavy paper

How to Sew a Pieced Sashing Table Runner

1 Straighten the cut edges of your fabrics, and trim off the selvages (page 33). Cut four 8½" (21.6 cm) squares from fabric A; also cut ten 4½" (11.5 cm) squares from fabric A. Cut 2½" (6.5 cm) strips from the entire crosswise width of each of the remaining fabrics; you'll need four strips of each if they are fat quarters or two strips of each if they are 45" (115 cm) wide.

(continued)

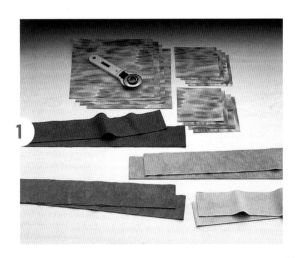

How to Sew a Pieced Sashing Table Runner continued

2 Arrange the strips of graduated colors in order from darkest to lightest. Place one strip from the first stack, right sides together, over a strip from the second stack, aligning the long edges. Stitch the strips together. Continue adding strips in graduated sequence from darkest to lightest.

TIP You can sew these strips together without pinning first if you take your time. Keep the edges aligned and hold both strips with even tension. The strips may not be exactly the same length. Start with the ends evenly aligned and begin stitching from that same end with each additional strip.

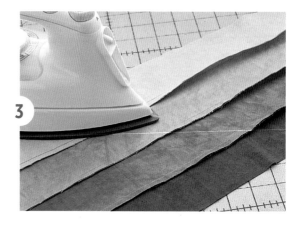

3 Sew the remaining strips into sets like the first one. Press all the seam allowances **toward the darker fabric (p. 83)**.

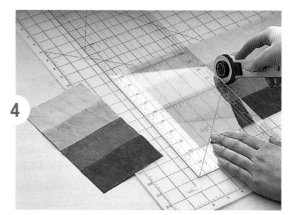

4 Cut the pieced fabric crosswise into 4½" (11.5 cm) strips. You will need a total of 13 pieced sashing strips.

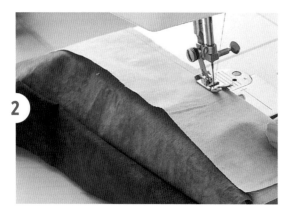

5 Arrange all of the pieces on a flat surface, and step back for a long look. There are many ways you might turn the sashing strips, causing the gradation of color to change direction. You may prefer an arrangement different from the one we have selected.

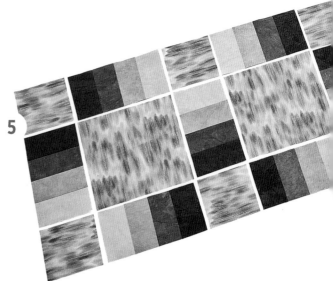

6 Stitch the long outer rows of sashing strips and connecting squares together, keeping the pieces in their arranged order. Press the new seam allowances toward the connecting squares. Return the sashing units to the surface.

7 Stitch the center row of sashing strips and large squares together, keeping the pieces in their arranged order. Press the new seam allowances toward the squares.

TIP Pin these pieces together first, one seam at a time, if you prefer. Stitch with the square on top, taking care to keep the seam allowances of the pieced strip turned in the direction they were pressed.

(continued)

6

7

8 Place the bottom sashing row along the lower edge of the center row, with right sides together, matching the seams. The seam allowances will be pressed in opposite directions at the seam intersections. **Insert a pin in the well of the seams (p. 83)**, to make sure they line up exactly. Stitch the rows together, **removing the pins as you come to them (p. 46)** and keeping the seam allowances turned in the proper directions.

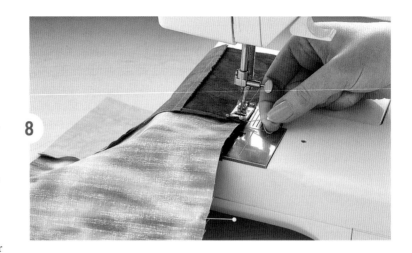

9 Stitch the remaining sashing row to the other side of the center row, as in step 8. Press these long seam allowances toward the center row.

10 Cut a quilting template of the desired shape from heavy paper, approximately 2½" (6.5 cm) tall and wide. Center the template in a connecting square. Trace lightly around the pattern, using a **fabric marker (p. 69)**. Repeat for each of the connecting squares. Trace four intertwined motifs in each large square.

11 Cut the backing and batting 4" (10 cm) longer and wider than the table runner. Layer and baste the table runner (page 36). Quilt by machine, stitching in the ditch (page 43) of the lengthwise sashing seams and all the crosswise seams that run edge to edge. Use a walking foot (page 11).

12 Hand-quilt (page 41) over the marked motifs in each connecting square and in the large squares. Remove your basting stitches. Cut binding strips from fabric A, and bind the table runner (page 44).

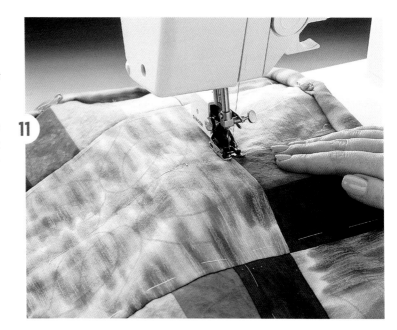

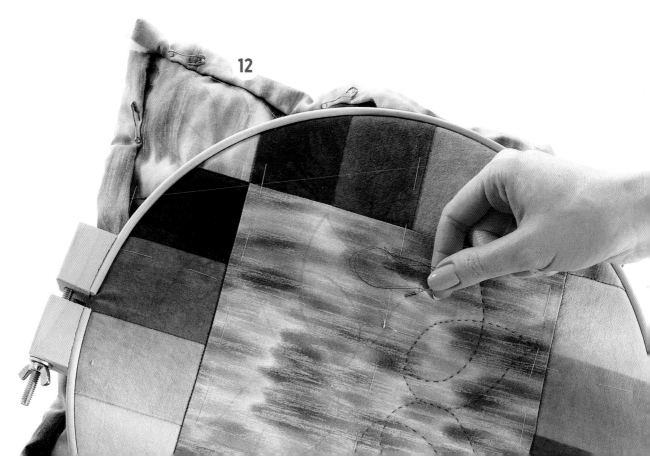

More Ideas

You can create a table runner for any special occa-
sion. Experiment and develop your own quilting
templates, or select from a wide range of templates
available at quilting shops.

Try your hand at selecting small print fabrics in
graduated color values (A and B) for the sashing.
Use a value tester (page 29), available at quilt
shops, to help you choose.

Select four sashing colors drawn from the
multicolored print used in the large and small
squares (C).

Hand-quilt the entire table runner, if you prefer.
Instead of machine stitching in the ditch, quilt by
hand ¼" (6 mm) inside the seam around each large
square (B).

A

B

C

Flannel Lap Quilt

Create a little coziness for cool evenings with this flannel lap quilt. Begin your fabric selection with a multicolor medium-size print flannel for the sashing and borders. Then, for the strip-pieced sections, select six flannels in colors to coordinate with the print. Pick fabrics of various color values, some in solid colors and others in small prints. You will also need a flannel fabric for the backing. The easy choice would be to repeat one of the strip-piecing fabrics. Ample fabric amounts are given below because flannel may tend to shrink more than other cotton. All seam allowances are ¼" (6 mm). The finished lap quilt measures about 55" × 38½" (140 × 98 cm).

WHAT YOU'LL LEARN..............

- How to strip-piece a quilt top
- Flannel is easy to sew
- How to finish the outer edges with a seam instead of binding

WHAT YOU'LL NEED...............

- 1⅝ yd. (1.5 m) fabric, for the sashing and borders
- ⅝ yd. (0.6 m) each of six fabrics that coordinate with the sashing and borders
- 1⅞ yd. (1.75 m) fabric, for the backing (possibly repeat one of the other fabrics)
- Low-loft batting, about 58" × 49" (147 × 125 cm)
- Rotary cutter and mat
- Quilting ruler
- Thread

How to Sew a Flannel Lap Quilt

1 Straighten the cut ends of the fabric, and trim off the selvages (page 33). Cut two 3" (7.5 cm) strips from the entire crosswise grain of each of the six strip-piecing fabrics. Cut three 3½" × 45½" (9 × 116 cm) sashing strips **from the lengthwise grain (p. 112)** of the sashing/border fabric. Cut four 5½" (14 cm) border strips from the entire lengthwise grain of the sashing/border fabric.

(continued)

How to Sew a Flannel Lap Quilt continued

QUICK REFERENCE

From the lengthwise grain. This eliminates the need to piece the sashing and border strips for the lap quilt.

2 Arrange six 3" (7.5 cm) strips in the order you would like to see them in your quilt. Place the first strip over the second strip, right sides together, aligning the long edges. Stitch the strips together. Then stitch the third strip to the other side of the second strip. Continue adding strips in sequence until you have sewn the complete six-strip unit.

TIP You can sew these strips together without pinning first, if you take your time. Keep the edges aligned and hold both strips with even tension. The strips may not be exactly the same length. Start with the ends evenly aligned and begin stitching from that same end with each additional strip.

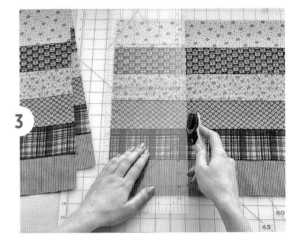

3 Sew the remaining strips into an identical six-strip unit. Press all the seam allowances in the same direction. Cut the six-strip units crosswise into 5½" (14 cm) strips. You will need a total of 12 pieced strips. Discard any excess fabric.

4 Stitch three strips together, end to end, in the same sequence, to make one long 18-piece strip. Repeat until you have sewn four identical long strips. Press the new seam allowances in the same direction as the others.

5 Place one sashing strip and one pieced strip right sides together, matching the centers and ends. Pin along the length, easing in any excess fullness. Stitch the seam, removing pins as you come to them and keeping all the seam allowances turned in the same direction.

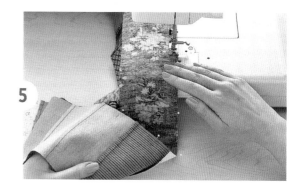

TIP It is easiest to sew this seam if the pieced strip is on the bottom, with the seam allowances pressed toward you.

6 Stitch another pieced strip to the other side of the sashing. Continue until you have stitched all the pieced strips and sashing strips together. Press all the seam allowances toward the sashing strips.

7 *Measure the quilt top across the middle* *(p. 45)*. Cut two of the border strips equal to this measurement. Pin one strip to the top of the quilt; pin the other strip to the bottom. Align the ends of the strips to the outer edges of the quilt top. Stretch the strips or the quilt slightly, if necessary, to make them fit. Stitch ¼" (6 mm) seams; press the seam allowances toward the borders.

(continued)

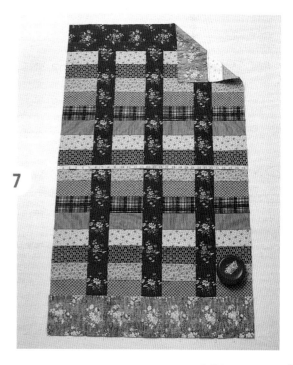

How to Sew a Flannel Lap Quilt continued

8 Measure the quilt top down the middle. Cut the remaining border strips equal to this measurement. Pin a strip to each side of the quilt, aligning the ends of the strips to the edges of the quilt top. Stretch the strips or the quilt slightly, if necessary, to make them fit. Stitch ¼" (6 mm) seams; press the seam allowances toward the borders.

9 Place the quilt top over the backing fabric, and trim the backing fabric to the same size. Layer both pieces, with the backing fabric on top, over the batting. Pin the layers together around the outer edge, using safety pins.

10 With the backing on top, stitch around the quilt ¼" (6 mm) from the edges, leaving a 10" (25.5 cm) opening for turning. Be sure to keep the raw edges of the quilt top and backing even. Trim the batting to ⅛" (3 mm). Trim the corners diagonally, to remove excess bulk. Insert a seam roll or hard cardboard tube into the opening, and place it under the outer seam. Press the seam allowances open.

11 Turn the quilt right side out through the opening. Press lightly around the outer edges. Slipstitch the opening closed, alternating small stitches from one side of the opening to the other.

12 Smooth the quilt out on a flat surface. Baste with safety pins, securing all three layers. Attach a walking foot (page 11). Quilt the lap quilt by stitching in the ditch (page 43) of the border seam. Then stitch in the ditch of the seams between the sashing and the pieced strips, beginning with the center rows and working outward. Remove the safety pins, and you're ready to cuddle up on the sofa with your new lap quilt!

Rail Fence Wall Hanging

Rectangles can be found in dozens of block quilt designs. Here they're combined in the Rail Fence pattern to create a dynamic wall hanging. A light-to-dark progression of four fabrics accentuates the quilt's zigzag pattern. Select four small prints with color values that progress from dark to light. Or select two solids and two prints that give the same effect. A two-color border, using the two darkest fabrics, creates the illusion of a mat and frame.

All of the seam allowances for this project are ¼" (6 mm). Sew as accurately as possible to ensure perfectly matched seams. The finished size is about 38½" × 30½" (98 × 77 cm).

WHAT YOU'LL LEARN

- Strip-piecing techniques
- How to sew a quilt with a double border
- How color arrangement creates optical illusions

WHAT YOU'LL NEED

- ⅜ yd. (0.35 m) fabric A (very light)
- ⅜ yd. (0.35 m) fabric B (light)
- ½ yd. (0.5 m) fabric C (medium)
- 1⅝ yd. (1.5 m) fabric D (dark)
- 1¼ yd. (1.15 m) of muslin, for backing and hanging sleeve
- Batting, about 42" × 32" (107 x81.5 cm)
- Rotary cutter and mat
- Quilting ruler
- Thread
- Sealed wood lath for hanging the quilt

How to Sew a Rail Fence Wall Hanging

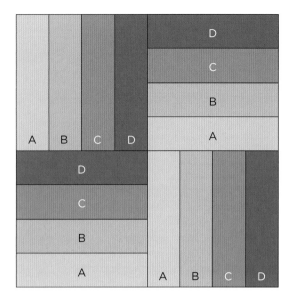

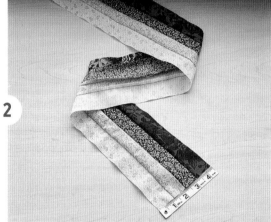

1 Straighten the cut ends of the fabric, and trim off the selvages (page 33). Cut six 1½" (3.8 cm) strips from the entire crosswise width of each of the four fabrics. Arrange the strips in four stacks (A to D) according to their color value, from lightest to darkest.

2 Pin an A strip and a B strip right sides together, aligning the long edges; ***insert the pins perpendicular to the long edge (p. 46)***. Stitch the strips together, ***removing the pins as you come to them (p. 46)***. Then stitch a C strip to the other side of the B strip, in the same manner. Add a D strip to the other side of the C strip. You should now have a pieced set, 4½" (11.5 cm) wide.

3 Repeat step 2 until you have six sets of pieced strips. Press all the seam allowances toward the darkest strips. Cut the strips, perpendicular to the seams, into 4½" (11.5 cm) squares. You should be able to cut at least nine squares from each set; you will need a total of 48 squares to make the wall hanging.

4 Stitch two squares, right sides together, in vertical-horizontal arrangement, with the darkest strips at the right and top. Press the seam allowances toward the vertical dark strip.

5 Stitch two more squares, right sides together, in horizontal-vertical arrangement, with the darkest strips at the top and right. Press the seam allowances toward the vertical light strip.

TIP Be sure to keep the fabrics in the same sequence from left to right and top to bottom throughout the quilt.

6 Stitch the two sets, right sides together and seams aligned. *Insert a pin in the wells of the seams (p. 83)*, to make sure they line up exactly. Stitch them together, removing the pins as you come to them and keeping the seam allowances turned in the opposite directions. Press the seam allowance toward the lower set.

(continued)

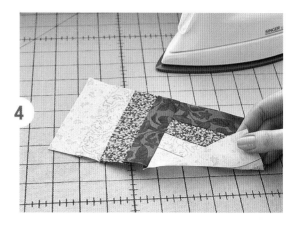

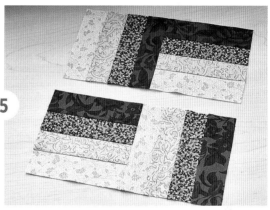

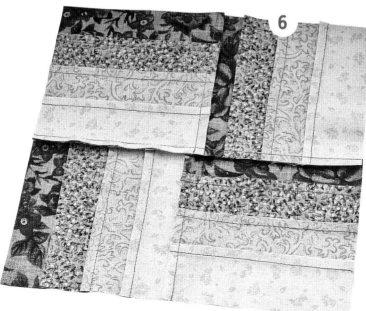

How to Sew a Rail Fence Wall Hanging *continued*

7 Repeat steps 4 to 6 until you have assembled 12 identical blocks. Arrange them in four rows of three blocks, on a flat surface. Stitch each horizontal row of blocks together, matching the seams and keeping the seam allowances turned in the direction they were pressed. Press the seam allowances in the top and third rows toward one side; press the seam allowances in the second and fourth rows in the opposite direction (note arrows). Return them to the flat surface.

8 Place the top two rows right sides together, aligning sea inue until you have stitched all four rows together.

> **TIP** Press the quilt top lightly from the right side and then return it to the flat surface. Now, stand back and let your eyes play for a while over the nifty zigzag pattern you have created.

9 Cut four 1½" (3.8 cm) strips from the entire crosswise width of fabric C, for the inner border. ***Measure the quilt top across the middle (p. 45).*** Cut two of the border strips equal to this measurement. Pin one strip to the top of the quilt; pin the other strip to the bottom. Align the ends of the strips to the outer edges of the quilt top. Stretch the strips or the quilt slightly, if necessary, to make them fit. Stitch ¼" (6 mm) seams; press the seam allowances toward the borders.

10 Measure the quilt top down the middle. Cut the two side border strips equal to this measurement. Pin a strip to each side of the quilt, aligning the ends of the strips to the edges of the quilt top. Stretch the strips or the quilt slightly, if necessary, to make them fit. Stitch ¼" (6 mm) seams; press the seam allowances toward the borders.

11 Cut four 2½" (6.5 cm) strips from the entire crosswise width of fabric D, for the outer border. Measure for and apply the outer borders in the same manner as the inner borders.

12 Cut the backing fabric and batting 4" (10 cm) longer and wider than the quilt top. Layer and baste the quilt (page 36). Attach a walking foot (page 11). Quilt by stitching in the ditch (page 43), *following this sequence (p. 91)*: Begin with a diagonal path near the center, stitching along both sides of the darkest zigzagging strip. Then stitch around both border seams. Finish quilting the remaining zigzagging strips. Bind the quilt (page 44). Add a sleeve for hanging, following steps 20 to 23 on page 169.

Log Cabin Sewing Machine Cover

Designed to fit most standard sewing machines, this cover features the ever-popular Log Cabin quilt block pattern. Eight Log Cabin blocks form the front, top, and back of the cover.

To create an interesting visual effect in the Log Cabin pattern, select two sets of contrasting colors, three of one and four of the other, in color values that progress from dark to light. They can be small prints, solids, or a mixture of both. In the photo at left and in the diagram on page 124, note how the color values, moving from the outer rectangles inward, progress from dark to light. The lightest fabric in the center square is also used for the side borders, ends, and binding of the sewing machine cover.

Chainstitching methods are used for quick and easy piecing of the eight blocks. All of the seam allowances for the project are ¼" (6 mm).

WHAT YOU'LL LEARN...

- How to make color values work for visual effect in a quilt pattern
- Chainstitching methods for quick and easy piecing of several identical blocks
- The importance of accuracy in cutting and piecing

WHAT YOU'LL NEED...

- ½ yd. (0.5 m) fabric A for borders, binding, and center squares
- ⅛ yd. (0.15 m) fabrics B, C, and D; ¼ yd. (0.25 m) fabrics E, F, and G, as described above
- 1 yd. (0.95 m) muslin for backing
- Low-loft batting, about 20″ × 32″ (51 × 81.5 cm)
- Rotary cutter and mat
- Quilting ruler
- Thread to blend with the fabrics

How to Sew a Log Cabin Sewing Machine Cover

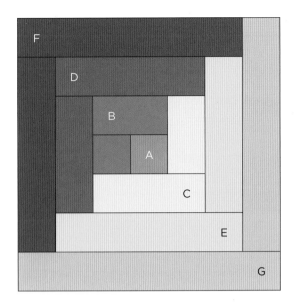

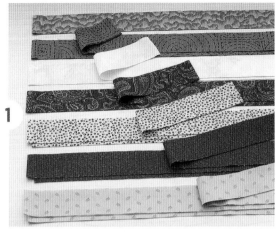

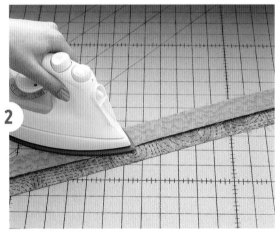

1 Straighten the cut ends of the fabrics, and trim away the selvages (page 33). Cut 1½" (3.8 cm) strips from the entire crosswise width of each fabric; you will need one strip of A, two strips of B, C, and D, three strips of E, F, and G. Arrange the strips in the order they will be used, from A to G, as in the diagram above.

2 Place strip A over strip B, right sides together, aligning the long edges. Stitch the strips together, keeping the edges aligned and holding both strips with even tension; they may not be exactly the same length. Press the seam allowances toward strip B.

3 Cut across the pieced strip at 1½" (3.8 cm) intervals, cutting eight sets. The lighter square of each of these sets will become the center of each Log Cabin block.

4 Place one set over a B strip, right sides together, aligning the ends and long edges. Position the set so that the A square is at the top; the seam allowance is turned down. Stitch them together. Without removing the fabric from the machine, place another set over the strip, aligning the edges and leaving a small space between sets. Stitch the second set in place.

5 Continue adding sets, leaving small spaces between them, until you have sewn all eight sets to the B strip. Place the pieced strip on the cutting mat, with the B strip on the bottom. Cut the sets apart, cutting the B strip even with the cut edges of the sets.

6 Press the seam allowances away from the center (A) squares.

7 Stitch a three-piece set to a C strip in the same manner. Position the set with the most recently added rectangle on the bottom; you will be crossing the most recently stitched seam, keeping those seam allowances turned away from the center square. Continue adding sets, leaving small spaces between them, until you have sewn all eight sets to the C strip.

(continued)

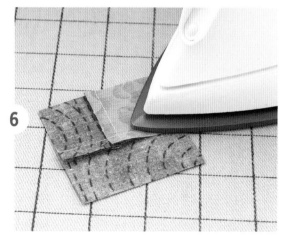

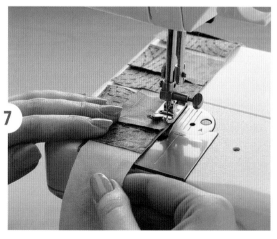

How to Sew a Log Cabin Sewing Machine Cover continued

8 Place the pieced strip on the cutting mat, with the C strip on the bottom. Cut the sets apart, cutting the C strip even with the edges of the three-piece sets. Press the seam allowances away from the center (A) squares.

9 Stitch a four-piece set to a C strip in the same manner. Position the set so that the most recently added rectangle is on the bottom; you will be crossing the most recently stitched seam, keeping those seam allowances turned away from the center square.

10 Continue adding sets, leaving small spaces between them, until you have sewn all eight sets to the C strip. Place the pieced strip on the cutting mat, with the C strip on the bottom. Cut the sets apart, cutting the C strip even with the edges of the four-piece sets. Press the seam allowances away from the center.

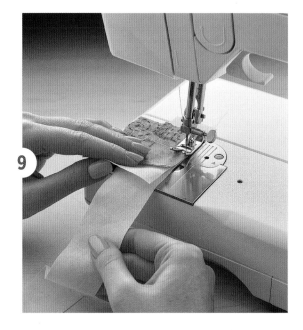

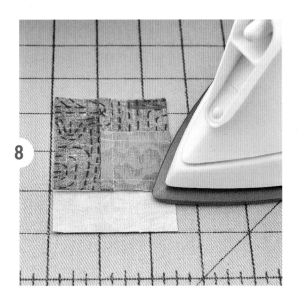

11 Have you got the idea? Continue building the blocks with this chainstitching method, adding two rectangles of each fabric in turn. Refer to the diagram on page 124 if you get confused. Sew accurate ¼" (6 mm) seams. Your squares should measure 7½" (19 cm).

TIP At any point, if you run out of strip length, take another strip of the same fabric and continue piecing.

12 Arrange all of the pieces on a flat surface, and step back for a long look. There are a few different ways you might turn the blocks to get the visual effect you want. Follow our example, or create a new pattern of your own.

13 Stitch each two-block row together. You may find it helpful to pin first, before stitching. Press the seam allowances in alternating directions from row to row (see arrows).

(continued)

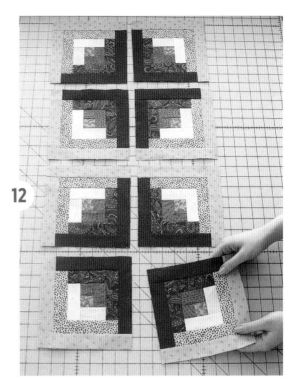

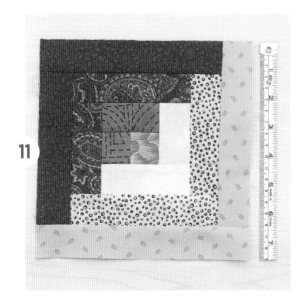

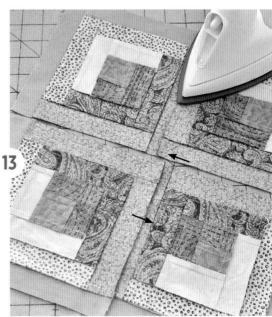

How to Sew a Log Cabin Sewing Machine Cover *continued*

14 Place the bottom two rows right sides together, matching the center seams. **Insert pins in the wells of the seams (p. 83).** Stitch the rows together, easing in any fullness; remove the pins as you come to them. Take care to keep all the seam allowances turned in the direction they were pressed. Add the remaining rows, one at a time. Your pieced section should measure 28½" × 14½" (72 × 37 cm).

15 Cut two 5½" (14 cm) strips from the entire crosswise width of fabric A. Cut the strips into two 28½" (72 cm) lengths for the side borders. Pin one strip to each side of the pieced section. Align the ends of the strips to the ends of the section, easing them to fit. Stitch ¼" (6 mm) seams; press the seam allowances toward the borders. Mark lines for channel quilting (page 43) 1" (2.5 cm) apart on the borders, beginning 1" (2.5 cm) from the seam. The last lines will be ¼" (6 mm) from the edge.

16 Cut the muslin backing and the batting 4" (10 cm) longer and wider than the pieced fabric. Layer and baste the quilt, as on page 36. Quilt by machine, stitching in the ditch (page 43) of the seams between the blocks and along the borders. Then **stitch diagonally (p. 101)** through the blocks. Channel-quilt the borders (page 43). Stitch around the outside, **a scant ¼" (6 mm) from the edge (p. 68).**

14

15

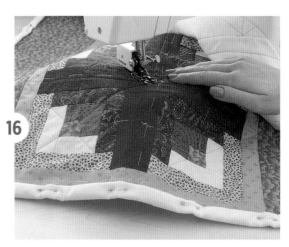

16

17 Trim the batting and the backing even with the top layer on the long sides. Do not trim the short ends. Fold the quilted piece in half crosswise, aligning the border edges; pin. Stitch the sides, ¼" (6 mm) from the edges. Finish the seam allowances together, using a zigzag stitch.

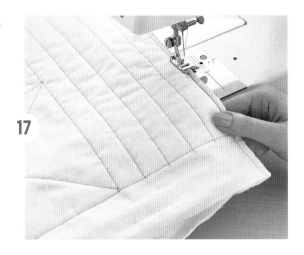

18 At an upper corner, separate the front and back, forming a triangle, with the seam in the center. Mark a line 3" (7.5 cm) below the point, *perpendicular to the seam*. Pin along the line through all the layers; stitch, removing the pins as you sew. Trim off the point ¼" (6 mm) from the seam, and finish the seam allowances together. Repeat for the opposite side.

19 Bind the lower edge, following the general directions on page 44, steps 5 to 9. In step 5, fold back the beginning end of the binding ½" (1.3 cm) and overlap the other end, forming a complete circle.

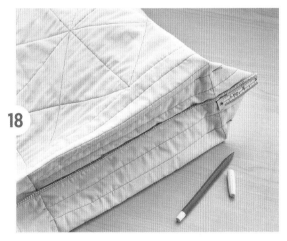

> ### QUICK REFERENCE
>
> *Perpendicular to the seam.* If your triangle is symmetrical, your marked line should be 6" (15 cm) long. The height of the cover, from each end of the line to the bottom edge, should be 11" (28 cm).

Ohio Star Flange Pillow

Triangles are frequently used in quilt blocks. This pattern, called the Ohio Star, is made from both squares and triangles, and requires only three different fabrics. The quilt block itself is 12" (30.5 cm) square, perfect for a small pillow. The border around the block becomes the pillow flange. The pillow back, sewn from the same fabric as the border, features a lapped closure for easy insertion and removal of the pillow form.

Select a multicolor print for the center square, the border flange, and the pillow back. Draw colors from the print, in either solid colors or small prints, to repeat in the star points and the background pieces that complete the block.

WHAT YOU'LL LEARN . . . .

- How to cut triangles
- How to chainstitch triangles
- How to make a flange pillow
- How to sew a lapped closure

WHAT YOU'LL NEED . . . .

- 1 yd. (0.95 m) fabric A, for the center square, border flange, and pillow back
- ⅜ yd. (0.35 m) each of two fabrics, for the star points and background
- ½ yd. (0.5 m) muslin, for backing
- 4" (10 cm) of ¾" (2 cm) hook and loop tape, for the closure
- Low-loft batting, about 22" (56 cm) square
- Rotary cutter and mat
- Quilting ruler
- 12" (30.5 cm) square pillow form
- Thread to match or blend with the fabrics

How to Sew an Ohio Star Flange Pillow

1 Straighten the cut ends of the fabric, and trim off the selvages (page 33). Cut two 3" (7.5 cm) strips from the entire crosswise width of fabric A for the border flange strips. Also cut two 12" × 19" (30.5 × 48 cm) rectangles for the pillow backs and one 4½" (11.5 cm) square from fabric A. Cut four 4½" (11.5 cm) squares and two 5½" (14 cm) squares from the background fabric. Cut two 5½" (14 cm) squares from the star point fabric.

(continued)

How to Sew an Ohio Star Flange Pillow continued

2 Layer the two larger background squares and the two star point squares, matching the raw edges. Cut through the squares diagonally in both directions, cutting them into triangles.

3 Align one star point triangle with one background triangle, right sides together. Stitch along one short side, taking care not to stretch the bias edges. Repeat for the remaining seven sets of triangles, chainstitching one right after the other, without cutting the thread. Place the fabrics in each set in the same position, and stitch the same edges.

4 Clip the sets apart. **Do not press them**. Place two sets right sides together, alternating fabrics. With your fingers, press the seam allowances toward the darker fabric. Pin the pieces together along the long edge, **inserting the pins in the wells of the seams (p. 83)**.

5 Stitch the long seam, taking care not to stretch the bias edges and keeping the seam allowances turned in the direction they were finger-pressed.

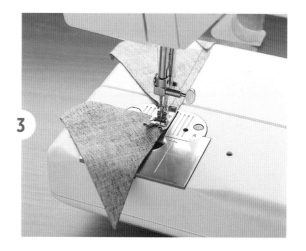

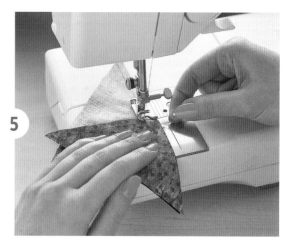

6 Repeat steps 4 and 5 for the remaining three sets, chainstitching one right after the other, without cutting the thread. Place the fabrics in each set in the same position, and stitch the same edges.

7 Clip the sets apart. Press the seams to one side. Trim off the points at the corners even with the sides.

8 Arrange the squares on a flat surface in the order shown. Stitch each horizontal row together. Press the seam allowances in the two outer rows away from the center square; press the seam allowances in the center row toward the center square.

QUICK REFERENCE

Do not press them. At this point, pressing would distort the shape of the pieces because they have been stitched on the bias.

(continued)

6

7

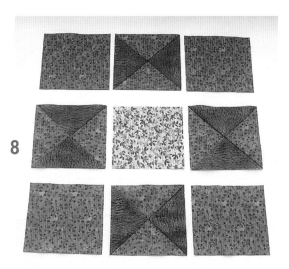

8

9 Pin the vertical rows together, inserting the pins in the wells of the seams. Stitch the rows together, keeping the seam allowances turned in the direction they were pressed. Press the new seam allowances toward the center.

10 **Measure the block across the middle (p. 45).** Cut two border strips equal to this measurement. Pin one strip to the top of the block; pin the other strip to the bottom. Align the ends of the strips to the sides of the block. Stretch the strips or the block slightly, if necessary, to make them fit. Stitch ¼" (6 mm) seams; press the seam allowances toward the borders.

11 Measure the block in the opposite direction across the center, including the new borders. Cut two remaining border strips equal to this measurement. Pin a strip to each side of the block, aligning the ends of the strips to the top and bottom edges of the block. Stretch the strips or the block slightly, if necessary, to make them fit. Stitch ¼" (6 mm) seams; press the seam allowances toward the borders.

9

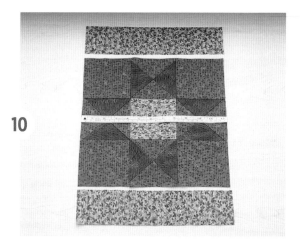

10

11

12 Cut muslin backing and the batting 4"
(10 cm) larger than the pillow top. Layer
and baste the pillow top as on page 36. Attach a
walking foot (page 11). Quilt the pillow top, stitching in the ditch (page 43) of the seam around the
center square. Then stitch four diagonal lines
through the triangle-pieced squares, beginning
and ending at the border seam for each line. Stitch
a scant ¼" (6 mm) from the outer edge (p. 68) of
the border. Trim the batting and backing even with
the top layer.

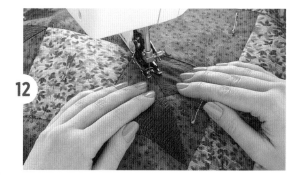

13 Press under 2" (5 cm) along one long edge
of a back rectangle. Unfold the pressed
edge. Turn the cut edge back, aligning it to the
first foldline; press the outer fold.

14 Unfold the hem edge. Center the hook side
of the hook and loop tape on the right side
of the fabric, between the two pressed folds. Secure
the tape, using a glue stick.

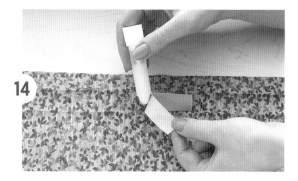

15 *Edgestitch* around the hook tape. At the
corners, stop with the needle down in the
fabric, and pivot. Overlap the stitches about ½" (1.3
cm) where they meet.

(continued)

:::
QUICK REFERENCE

Edgestitch. Stitch as close as possible to the edge of the
tape. Align the presser foot so that the needle will enter
the tape just inside the outer edge. Determine the point
on the presser foot that aligns to the outer edge of the
tape. As you sew, rather than watching the needle, watch
the edge of the tape pass under that point on the presser
foot. Stitch slowly for best control.
:::

16 Refold hem along the pressed foldlines, encasing raw edge, to form a 1" (2.5 cm) double-fold hem. Pin the hem, inserting the pins perpendicular to the folds.

17 Place the pinned hem under the presser foot of the machine, with the wrong side of the pillow back facing up and the needle aligned to enter the fabric just inside the inner fold. Stitch along the fold.

18 Follow step 13 for the second pillow back piece. Pin the folded hem in place. Then follow step 17. Center the loop side of the hook and loop tape on the right side of the hemmed piece, between the fold and the stitching line. Secure the tape, using a glue stick.

19 Edgestitch around the loop tape, pivoting at the corners and overlapping the stitches about ½" (1.3 cm) where they meet.

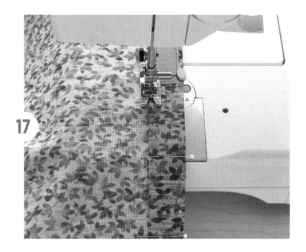

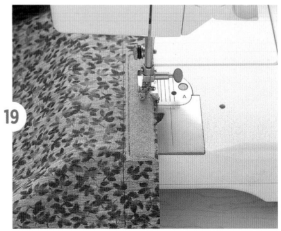

20 Overlap the two pillow back pieces so the foldline of the upper piece aligns to the stitching line of the lower piece. Seal the hook and loop tape. Trim the pillow back to the same size as the front. Pin the raw edges together on each side where the hems overlap.

21 Pin the pillow front to the pillow back, right sides together. Attach a walking foot (page 11). Stitch completely around the four sides *¼" (6 mm) from the edges (p. 68)*. Overlap the stitches about ½" (1.3 cm) where they meet. Trim the seam allowances diagonally at the four corners to remove excess bulk.

22 Turn the pillow cover right side out. Use a point turner or similar tool to carefully push the corners out, if necessary. Press lightly. Pin the layers together along the border seam, inserting the pins perpendicular to the sides.

23 Stitch in the ditch of the border seam, creating the pillow flange. Remove pins as you come to them. Stop stitching with the needle down in the fabric to pivot at the corners. Overlap the stitches ½" (1.3 cm) where they meet. Now simply insert the pillow form and close the opening.

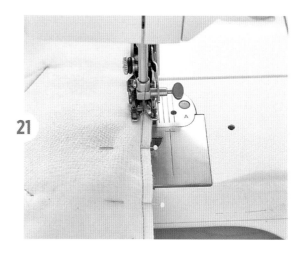

21

22

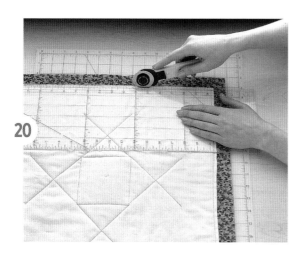

20

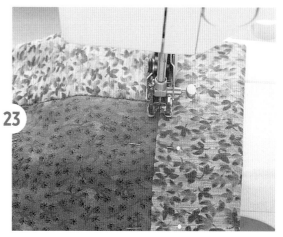

23

Churn Dash Wall Hanging

The simple nine-patch blocks of this Amish-style quilt are made of squares, rectangles, and triangles. The design, symbolic of the mixing movements of an antique butter churn, is created in black fabric and set off by solid, bold, background colors. The triple border frames the design to perfection. Continuous diagonal quilting lines trace the outer corners of all the churn dash blocks and keep the eye moving over the surface of the quilt.

WHAT YOU'LL LEARN . . . .

- How to piece a nine-patch block using a variety of shapes
- How to sew a quilt with multiple borders
- How to mark quilting lines on a quilt top

WHAT YOU'LL NEED . . . .

- ⅝ yd. (0.6 m) black fabric for churn dash design and second border
- ¼ yd. (0.25 m) each of three bold background fabrics
- 1⅓ yd. (1.27 m) for sashing, first and third borders, and binding
- Rotary cutter and mat
- Quilting ruler
- 1⅛ yd. (1.05 m) muslin for backing and hanging sleeve
- Low-loft batting, about 38" (96.5 cm) square
- Thread to match or blend with the fabrics
- Sealed wood lath for hanging the quilt

How to Sew a Churn Dash Wall Hanging

1 Straighten the cut edges of the fabrics and trim off the selvages (page 33). Cut two 2⅞" (7.2 cm) strips on the crosswise grain of the black fabric. From the strips, cut 18 2⅞" (7.2 cm) squares. Cut the squares in half diagonally to make 36 triangles. Also from the black fabric, cut two 2½" (6.5 cm) strips on the crosswise grain. From the strips, cut 36 1½" × 2½" (3.8 × 6.5 cm) rectangles. (You may have to cut a few of the rectangles from strips left over after cutting the squares.)

(continued)

2 Cut 36 triangles and 36 rectangles from the background fabrics (12 of each color) in the same sizes as the black ones cut in step 1. Cut three 2½" (6.5 cm) squares from each of the background colors for the centers of the blocks.

3 Cut seven 2½" (6.5 cm) strips on the cross-wise grain for the sashing and first border. Cut one strip into six 6½" (16.5 cm) pieces for vertical sashing. From the same fabric, cut four 3½" (9 cm) strips on the crosswise grain for the third border and four 3" (7.5 cm) strips for binding. Cut four 1½" (3.8 cm) strips on the crosswise grain of the black fabric for the second border.

4 Place one design and one background triangle, right sides together, aligning all the edges. Stitch ¼" (6 mm) from the long edge, taking care not to stretch the bias edges. Repeat for the remaining 35 pairs, chainstitching one right after the other, without cutting the thread.

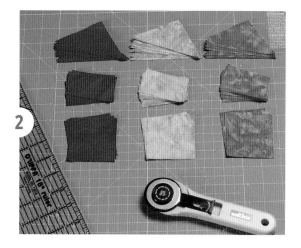

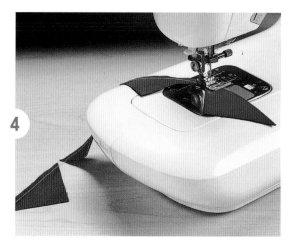

5 Place one design and one background rectangle, right sides together, aligning all the edges. Stitch ¼" (6 mm) from one long edge. Repeat for the remaining 35 rectangle pairs, chain-stitching one right after the other, without cutting the thread.

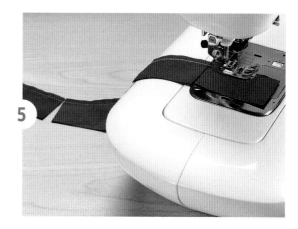

6 Clip the triangle and rectangle pairs apart. Press the seam allowances toward the black fabric. Trim off the points that extend beyond the corners of the triangle-pieced squares.

7 Arrange the eight pieced squares around the plain center square for each block as shown. Stitch each row of blocks together. Finger-press the seam allowances of the top and bottom rows toward the center. Finger-press the seam allowances of the center row away from the center.

TIP Clip thread short at the beginning and end of each seam as you go along. This will keep the back of the block looking much neater and prevent long thread tails from getting caught up in the seams.

(continued)

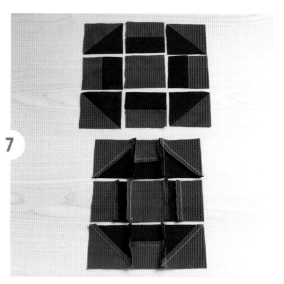

8 Place the top row over the middle row, right sides together, aligning the edges and seams. The seam allowances will be pressed in opposite directions. **Insert a pin in the wells of the seams (p. 83)**, to make sure they line up exactly. Stitch the rows together, **removing the pins as you come to them (p. 46)** and keeping the seam allowances turned in the opposite directions. Stitch the bottom row to the other side of the middle row in the same manner.

TIP As you approach seam allowances that have been pressed toward the presser foot, the raw edges may "buckle" under the front of the presser foot. Stop stitching with the needle down in the fabric, and raise the presser foot to allow the seam allowances to return to their pressed position. Use a long pin or the point of your seam ripper to coax them into place and hold them there while you lower the presser foot and continue stitching.

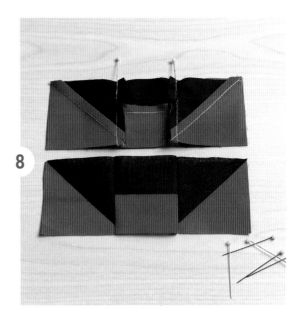

9 Repeat steps 7 and 8 for the remaining eight blocks. Press the blocks, turning the long seam allowances away from the middle.

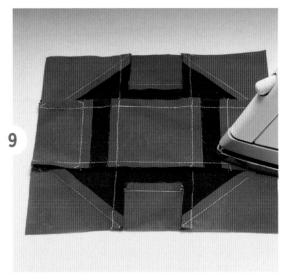

10 Arrange the blocks on a surface in three rows of three blocks, following the photo on page 138 or in an order of your own choosing. Place short sashing strips between the blocks in each row. Stitch the first row of sashing strips and blocks together, keeping the pieces in their arranged order. Align the ends of the strips to the upper and lower edges of the blocks, easing the blocks to fit as necessary. It is easiest to stitch with the sashing strip on top, keeping the seam allowances of the block turned in the direction they were pressed.

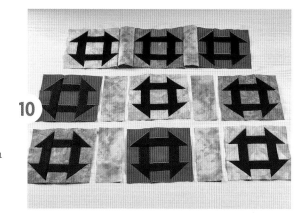

11 Repeat step 10 for the middle and bottom rows. Check to make sure that the outer points of the black triangles just touch the sashing. If any points are not right, remove the stitches for about 1" (2.5 cm) on each sides of the point, using the point of a seam ripper, and restitch them with the block on top so you can be sure the new stitching line intersects with the point. Press all the seam allowances toward the sashing strips.

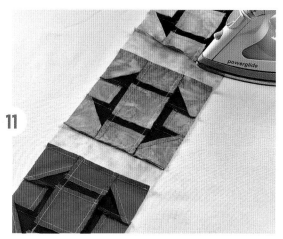

12 Return the rows to the work surface. Measure the rows. Cut two sashing strips and two inner border strips to the length of the shortest row. Pin the top border to the top of the top row, easing in fullness evenly. Stitch. Add the sashing to the bottom of the top row. Stitch a border and a sashing strip to the top and bottom of the bottom row.

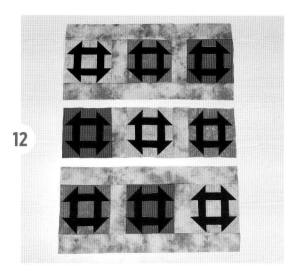

(continued)

How to Sew a Churn Dash Wall Hanging *continued*

13 Place a straightedge along the first seam between the sashing and block of the top row, extending across the sashing. Make a small mark on the unstitched edge of the sashing next to the straightedge. Repeat at each seam. Pin the middle row to the upper sashing, making sure that the seams align to the marks. Stitch. Join the lower row to the middle row in the same manner.

14 Check the points as in step 11. Correct any that are not perfect. Press the seam allowances toward the sashing and borders. Measure down the center of the quilt and cut the side borders to this length. Pin in place and stitch. Press seam allowances toward the borders.

15 Cut second border strips equal in length to the measurement across the middle of the quilt. Attach the top and bottom borders; press allowances toward the second border. Cut the side borders equal in length to the measurement down the center of the quilt. Attach the side borders; press seam allowances toward the second border.

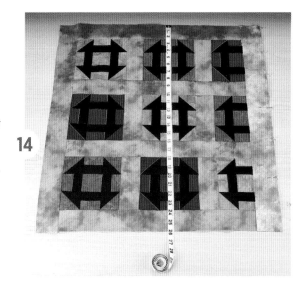

14

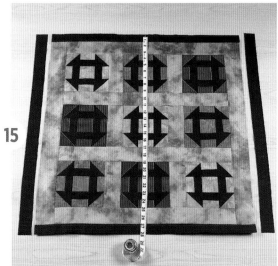

15

13

16 Repeat step 15 for the third border. Spread the quilt out on a flat surface. If you have stitched accurately, the diagonal lines of the churn dash corners will align diagonally across the quilt. You can easily "eyeball" the quilting path in the area of the blocks. Align a straightedge to a one of the diagonal lines and, using a quilt marking pencil, mark the lines extending over the borders. Repeat for the other diagonals in all directions.

17 Layer and baste the quilt as on page 36. Attach a walking foot (page 11). Thread the machine with thread that matches the outer border. Machine-quilt by stitching in the ditch (page 43) of all the border seams. Then stitch along the horizontal sashings. When you quilt the vertical sashings, cross to the opposite side over the horizontal sashings, forming an X at the block corners. Finish by quilting the diagonal lines. Bind the edges, following the directions on page 44. Make a sleeve for hanging the quilt, following steps 20 to 23 on page 167.

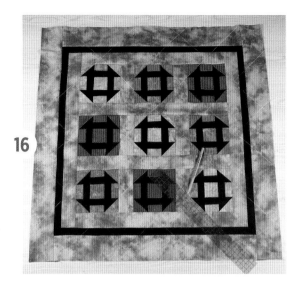

16 ⟩

17 ⟩

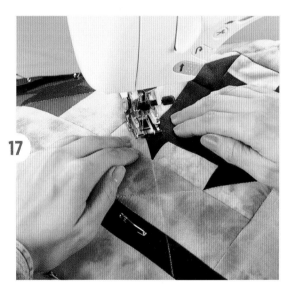

Flying Geese Doll Blanket

Pretty triangles, lined up in rows, echo the V pattern formed by geese as they fly across the sky. Quilted up in dainty pastels, this doll blanket is an exercise in sewing triangles on the bias. The finished size of the blanket is 22" × 16" (56 × 40.5 cm), just right for the popular 18" (46 cm) doll size. Instead of binding, the quilt top is lined to the edge with the backing fabric. Because of its size, this is an easy project to machine-quilt. Even hand-quilting wouldn't take much time. Select a small-scale multicolor floral print fabric for the sashing border, and backing. Then, drawing colors from the print, select three tiny-grained prints in different color values for the "geese" and a white or off-white for the "sky" around them.

WHAT YOU'LL LEARN. . . . .

- How to chainstitch triangles on the bias
- The best way to press bias seam allowances
- How to line to the edge

WHAT YOU'LL NEED. . . . .

- ¾ yd (0.7 m) small-scale multicolor print for sashing, borders, and backing
- ¼ yd. (0.25 m) each of three tiny-grained fabrics for geese
- ¼ yd. (0.25 m) white or off-white fabric for sky
- Extra-low-loft batting, about 23 × 17 (58.5 × 43 cm)
- Rotary cutter and mat
- Quilting ruler
- White or off-white thread
- Yarn or pearl cotton in colors to match geese, for tying quilt
- Large-eyed hand-sewing needle for tying quilt

How to Sew a Flying Geese Doll Blanket

1 Straighten the cut edges of the fabric and trim off the selvages (page 33). Cut one 5¼" (13.3 cm) strip from the entire crosswise grain of each of the three tiny-grained fabrics. Layer the strips and cut three stacks of 5¼" (13.3 cm) squares. Cut through each stack diagonally in both directions, cutting them into triangles. You will need ten triangles of each fabric. Cut two 2⅞" (7.2 cm) strips from the crosswise grain of the white fabric. Layer the strips and cut sets of fifteen 2⅞" (7.2 cm) squares. Cut each set of squares in half diagonally for a total of 60 triangles.

How to Sew a Flying Geese Doll Blanket *continued*

2 Align the long side of one white triangle to one short side of a colored triangle, right sides together. The points should match at the base of the large triangle. Stitch ¼" (6 mm) from the edge, taking care not to stretch the bias edges. Repeat for the remaining 29 geese, chainstitching one right after the other, without cutting the thread. Place the fabrics in each set in the same direction and stitch the same edges.

3 Clip the units apart. Press the seam allowances toward the small triangles. To avoid stretching the bias edges, move the iron in the direction of the grainline, from the base of the goose toward the point.

4 Stitch a small triangle to the other short side of the large triangle, right sides together, matching the points at the base of the large triangle. Repeat for the remaining 29 geese, chainstitching one after the other. Clip the units apart.

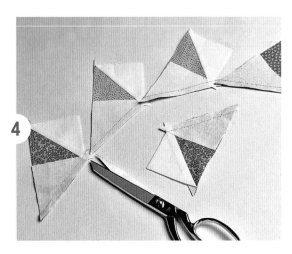

5 Press the seam allowances toward the small triangles, as in step 3. Trim off the points at the tops of the large triangles. Arrange the units on a flat surface in three columns of ten geese as shown.

6 Flip the top unit in the first column over onto the unit below it, right sides together. Turn the set over, so the large triangle of the second unit points to the right and all edges align. Stitch the units together, making sure that the new seam crosses the triangle point *at the exact point where the diagonal seams intersect*.

7 Replace the set on the surface, and continue adding units to the column, following step 6. Repeat for the left column. When you stitch the center column together, you don't have to turn the set over before stitching because the geese are flying in the opposite direction. Place a column facedown on the pressing surface, and slide the iron from one end to the other, pressing all the seam allowances toward the bases of the geese. Repeat for the other columns.

QUICK REFERENCE

At the exact point where the diagonal seams intersect.
This ensures that the full triangle will be displayed on the right side of the quilt top. If the diagonal seams were sewn accurately at ¼" (6 mm), the intersecting point should be ¼" (6 mm) from the edge. It's OK to cheat a little, if necessary to make the stitches intersect.

(continued)

How to Sew a Flying Geese Doll Blanket continued

8 Measure the lengths of the three pieced strips. From the printed fabric, cut three strips on the crosswise grain, 1½" (3.8 cm) wide. From two of the strips, cut pieces for the side borders and sashing equal in length to the shortest pieced strip. Set the other strip aside.

9 Place one sashing strip and one pieced strip right sides together, matching the centers and ends. Pin along the length, *inserting pins perpendicular to the edges (p. 46)* and easing in any excess fullness. Stitch the seam, *removing pins as you come to them (p. 46)* and keeping all the seam allowances turned in the direction they were pressed. Stitch the remaining sashing and side border strips to the pieced strips. Press the seam allowances toward the sashing and borders.

10 *Measure the quilt top across the middle (p. 45)*. Cut the top and bottom borders from the remaining 1½" (3.8 cm) strip equal in length to this measurement. Pin the top border strip to the top of the quilt, right sides together, matching the centers and ends. Pin along the length, easing in any excess fullness. Stitch the seam, removing pins as you come to them and keeping all the seam allowances turned in the direction they were pressed. Repeat for the bottom border. Press the seam allowances toward the borders.

8

9

10

11 Place the quilt top over the backing fabric, and trim the backing fabric to the same size. Repeat to cut the batting. Spray the batting with temporary fabric adhesive and apply it to the wrong side of the quilt top. Layer the backing over the quilt top, right sides together. Pin the layers together around the outer edges.

12 With the backing on top, stitch around the quilt ¼" (6 mm) from the edges, leaving a 6" (15 cm) opening for turning. Be sure to keep the raw edges of the quilt top and backing even. Trim the batting to ⅛" (3 mm). Trim the corners diagonally, to remove excess bulk. Turn the quilt right side out through the opening. Press lightly around the outer edges. Slipstitch (page 62, step 13) the opening closed.

13 Smooth the quilt out on a flat surface. Baste with safety pins in the goose columns, securing all three layers. Attach a walking foot (page 11). Machine-quilt by stitching in the ditch (page 43) of the border seam. Or quilt in the ditch by hand (page 41).

(continued)

How to Sew a Flying Geese Doll Blanket *continued*

14 To hand-tie the quilt, thread a large-eyed needle with a double strand of pearl cotton or yarn; don't tie a knot in the end. Take a tiny stitch at the point of the first goose in a column, catching the backing. Pull the strands through, leaving tails about 2" (5 cm) long.

15 Grasp the tails along with the other two strands between the thumb and index finger of your free hand. Wrap the needle end counterclockwise around the strands and up through the loop that forms.

16 Release the long strands and pull the knot tight to the surface. Trim all tails to the desired length. Tie the quilt at the points of all remaining geese triangles. Remove the safety pins.

More Flying Geese

Make a matching pillow, using three geese blocks sewn together in a row; add a narrow border. Use the border fabric for the backing. Follow steps 12 to 14 on page 85 for making the pillow. Stuff it with leftover bits of batting.

Star Sashing Baby Quilt

Sometimes a printed fabric is so darn cute, you hate to cut it up. For this baby quilt, sashing strips with connecting stars create splashes of bold color that perfectly complement the whole squares of an adorable kid-print fabric. Begin fabric selection by choosing an irresistible, multicolor print. Then, from the colors in the print, pick a solid dark color value fabric for the main sashing and borders. Choose three solid-color star fabrics that have medium to light values. The final dimensions of this baby quilt are about 35" × 42.5" (89 × 108 cm).

WHAT YOU'LL LEARN. . . . .

- How to sew precision triangles with ease
- How to match seams perfectly
- How to select perfectly color-coordinating fabrics for an exciting quilt

WHAT YOU'LL NEED. . . . .

- ⅝ yd. (0.6 m) multicolor print fabric
- 1 yd. (0.92 m) fabric for sashing strips, borders, and binding
- ¼ yd. (0.25 m) each of three fabrics for stars
- 1 yd. (0.92 m) fabric for backing
- Rotary cutter and mat
- Quilting ruler
- 1 yd. (0.92 m) low-loft batting
- Thread

How to Sew a Star Sashing Baby Quilt

1 Straighten the cut edges of your fabrics, and trim off the selvages (page 33). Cut three 6" (15 cm) strips of the multicolor print. From the strips, cut 20 6" (15 cm) squares. Cut five 2¾" (7 cm) strips of the sashing fabric; from the strips, cut 31 6" (15 cm) rectangles.

(continued)

How to Sew a Star Sashing Baby Quilt continued

2 Cut a 2¾" (7 cm) strip from each of the three star fabrics. From each strip, cut four 2¾" (7 cm) squares. Cut two 1⅝" (4 cm) strips from each of the three fabrics. From the strips, cut 32 1⅝" (4 cm) squares of each color.

3 Place a small star square in one corner of a sashing strip, with right sides together and raw edges even. Stitch diagonally as shown.

4 Press the square in half along the stitching line, so the outer edges align to the outer edges of the sashing strip. Trim off the the sashing and underlayer of star fabric at the corner, leaving ¼" (6 mm) seam allowances.

3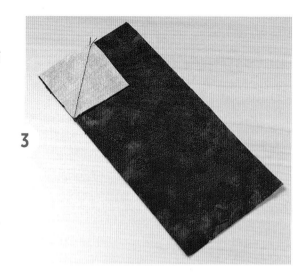

2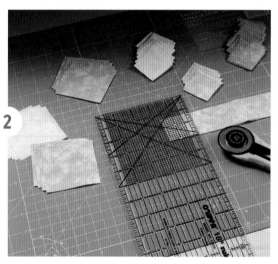

4

5 Repeat steps 3 and 4 on the other corner of the same end of the sashing strip. Prepare fourteen sashing strips with triangles at one end; five of each of two star colors and four of the remaining color. These will be used as end strips.

TIP If you find it difficult to stitch diagonally with accuracy, take the time to draw a light pencil line diagonally on the wrong side of each square. To save time, chainstitch the squares as in step 3 and then do all the pressing and trimming (step 4) at once.

6 Stitch triangles to all four corners of the remaining seventeen sashing strips, as in steps 3 and 4. Follow the photo in step 13 for color order. These will be used as inner strips.

7 Stitch three end strips between four 6" (15 cm) print squares, using ¼" (6 mm) seam allowances. Make sure all the plain ends align to the tops of the squares. This will be the top row of the quilt. Press the seam allowances toward the print squares. Repeat in the same color order to make a bottom row, with the plain ends of the strips aligned to the bottoms of the squares.

TIP To avoid confusion and help envision the quilt as it goes together, many quilters mount a large piece of cotton batting on the wall and arrange the pieces on it. (They will stay in place without pins.) The pieces are taken in order as they are stitched and then returned to the batting.

(continued)

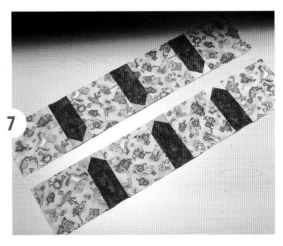

How to Sew a Star Sashing Baby Quilt *continued*

8 Stitch the three inner rows of the quilt together, using the sashing strips that have triangles at both ends, and following the photo in step 13 for color order. Press all the seam allowances toward the squares.

9 Stitch two end sashing strips and two inner strips alternately to the star squares for the first sashing row; follow the photo in step 13 for color order. Stitch with the pieced strips on top so you can make sure the stitches intersect exactly at the points. Press the seam allowances toward the squares. Repeat for the remaining three sashing rows.

10 Arrange all of the pieces on a flat surface. Pin the first row to the first sashing row, right sides together, matching seams. The seam allowances will be pressed in opposite directions at the seam intersections. ***Insert a pin in the wells of the seams (p. 83)***, to make sure they line up exactly. Stitch the rows together, ***removing pins as you come to them (p. 46)*** and keeping the seam allowances turned in the proper directions. Stitch with the block rows on top so you can make sure the stitches intersect exactly at the points. Continue adding rows until the entire quilt top is complete. Press all the new seam allowances toward the sashing.

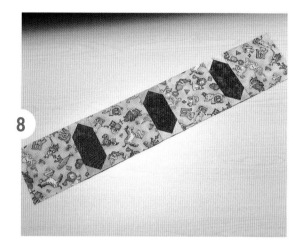

8

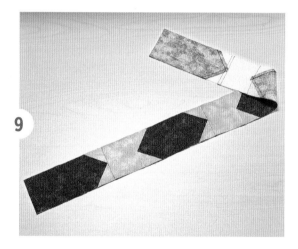

9

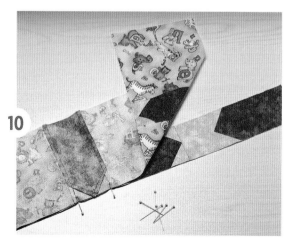

10

11 *Measure the quilt top across the middle (p. 45).* Cut two 3½" (9 cm) border strips equal to this measurement. Pin one strip to the top of the quilt; pin the other strip to the bottom. Align the ends of the strips to the outer edges of the quilt top. Stretch the strips or the quilt top slightly, if necessary, to make them fit. Stitch ¼" (6 mm) seams; press the seam allowances toward the borders.

12 Measure the quilt top down the middle. Cut the remaining border strips equal to this measurement. Pin a strip to each side of the quilt, aligning the ends of the strips to the edges of the quilt top. Stretch the strips or the quilt slightly, if necessary, to make them fit. Stitch ¼" (6 mm) seams; press the seam allowances toward the borders.

13 Cut the backing and batting 4" (10 cm) longer and wider than the quilt top. Layer and baste the quilt (page 36) . Attach a walking foot (page 11). Quilt by stitching in the ditch (page 43) around each large square, starting with the squares in the center row and working outward to the top and bottom. Bind the quilt, following the directions on page 44.

12

13
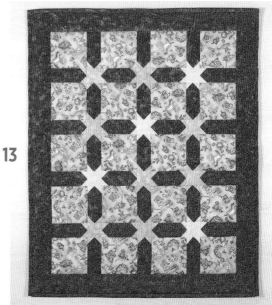

11
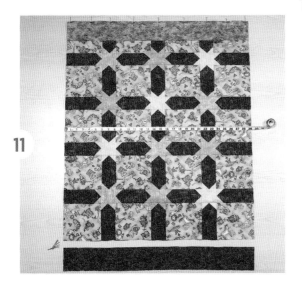

Bow Ties Wall Hanging

The Bow Tie block has been a favorite of quilters for centuries because of its symmetry and clean geometric lines. The block is made using a simplified method of quick cutting and chainstitching. Begin your fabric selection with a multicolored print for the borders and binding. Drawing colors from this print, select four small coordinating prints or a combination of prints and solids. The wall hanging shown here is made from 16 blocks of each bow tie color. Its finished size is about 37" (94 cm) square.

WHAT YOU'LL LEARN...

- How to choose several coordinating fabrics
- A new way to piece triangles
- The importance of accuracy in both cutting and piecing
- How to make a sleeve for a hanging quilt

WHAT YOU'LL NEED...

- ⅜ yd. (0.35 m) each of four fabrics A, B, C, and D, for bow ties
- ¾ yd. (0.7 m) background fabric
- ¾ yd. (0.6 m) fabric, for border and binding
- 1¼ yd. (1.15 m) muslin, for backing, plus 6" (15 cm), for hanging sleeve
- Low-loft batting, about 41" (104 cm) square
- Rotary cutter and mat
- Quilting ruler
- Thread that matches one of your fabrics or harmonizes with all of them
- Sealed wooden lath for hanging the quilt

How to Sew a Bow Ties Wall Hanging

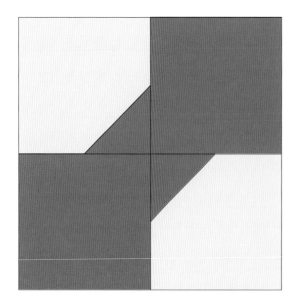

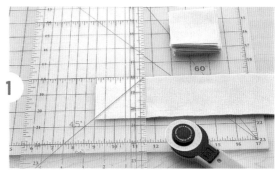

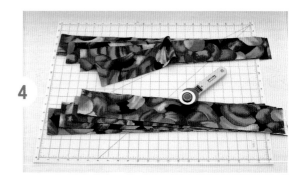

1 Straighten the cut ends of the fabric, and trim off the selvages (page 33). Cut eight 2½" (6.5 cm) strips from the entire crosswise width of the background fabric. From these strips, cut 128 2½" (6.5 cm) squares.

2 Cut two 2½" (6.5 cm) strips from the entire crosswise width of fabric A. From these strips, cut 32 2½" (6.5 cm) squares. Repeat for fabrics B, C, and D, cutting 32 squares of each fabric.

3 Cut two 1½" (3.8 cm) strips from the entire crosswise width of fabric A. From these strips, cut 32 1½" (3.8 cm) squares. Repeat for fabrics B, C, and D, cutting 32 squares of each fabric.

4 Cut eight 3" (7.5 cm) strips from the entire crosswise width of the border/binding fabric: four for the border and four for the binding.

5 Place a 1½" (3.8 cm) square in one corner of a background square, with right sides together and raw edges even. With the stitch length set at 10 to 12 stitches per inch, which equals 2.5 mm, stitch diagonally from corner to corner of the smaller square. Without cutting the thread or removing the first pieced square from the sewing machine bed, repeat this step with a second set of squares. Continue chainstitching in this manner until you have sewn all 128 sets of squares.

6 Lay out the chain of squares on the pressing surface. Press all the small squares in half along the stitched lines, matching the outer edges to the large square.

7 Flip the squares over. Trim the large square and one layer of the small square at the stitched corner, leaving ¼" (6 mm) seam allowance. Carefully clip all of the pieced squares apart.

8 With right sides together and raw edges aligned, join a pieced square to a large square of the same bow tie fabric, as shown. Stitch a ¼" (6 mm) seam. Use the chainstitching technique to join all the pieced squares in the same manner.

(continued)

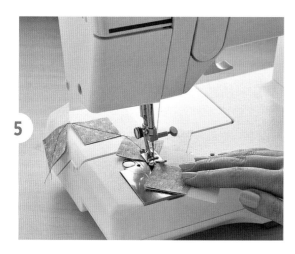

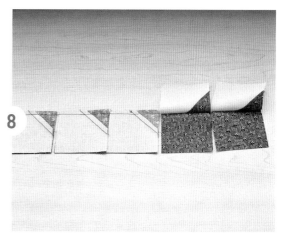

9 Lay out the chain of joined sets on the pressing surface. Press all the seam allowances toward the whole squares. Carefully clip all the sets apart.

10 Place two similar sets right sides together, aligning the seams at the center. The seam allowances will be pressed in opposite directions. **Insert a pin in the wells of the seams (p. 83),** to make sure they line up exactly. Stitch a ¼" (6 mm) seam, forming a Bow Tie block; remove the pin when you come to it. Use the chainstitching technique to join all the sets into Bow Tie blocks.

TIP For the first few sets, you may feel more comfortable pinning them together at the center seam. Once you get the rhythm, try stitching them together without the pin. Stitch slowly to ensure that the seams line up perfectly and the seam allowances stay pressed in opposite directions.

11 Lay out the chain of Bow Tie blocks on the pressing surface. Press all the seam allowances in the same direction. Carefully clip all the blocks apart.

9

10

11

12 Arrange the blocks on a flat surface as shown: eight across and eight down. The seams sewn in step 10 should run vertically, with their seam allowances pressed in alternate directions down each vertical row.

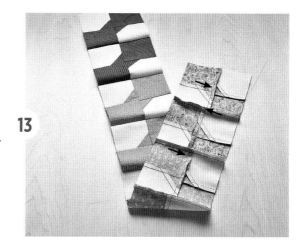

13 Join the blocks in one vertical row, stitching ¼" (6 mm) seams, beginning at the top. You should notice that all the aligning seam allowances are pressed in opposite directions (arrows). Press all the new seam allowances in the same direction. Replace the row on the surface.

14 Repeat step 13 for each vertical row, pressing the seam allowances of adjoining rows in opposite directions (arrows).

15 Pin the rows right sides together, aligning raw edges and seams. Again you will notice that all the aligning seam allowances are pressed in opposite directions. Stitch a ¼" (6 mm) seam, removing pins when you come to them.

(continued)

16 Press all the new seam allowances in the same direction (arrows). Lightly press the entire quilt top from the wrong side, then from the right side.

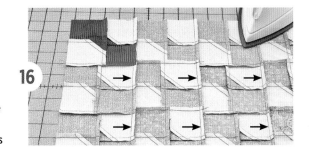

> **TIP** Now take a little breather. Stand back and admire your work. If you have sewn accurately, all your seams align, forming perfect intersections. That is quite an accomplishment!

17 *Measure the quilt top across the middle (p. 45)*. Cut two of the border strips equal to this measurement. Pin one strip to the top of the quilt; pin the other strip to the bottom. Align the ends of the strips to the outer edges of the quilt top. Stretch the strips or the quilt slightly, if necessary, to make them fit. Stitch ¼" (6 mm) seams; press the seam allowances toward the borders.

18 Measure the quilt top down the middle. Cut the remaining border strips equal to this measurement. Pin a strip to each side of the quilt, aligning the ends of the strips to the edges of the quilt top. Stretch the strips or the quilt slightly, if necessary, to make them fit. Stitch ¼" (6 mm) seams; press the seam allowances toward the borders.

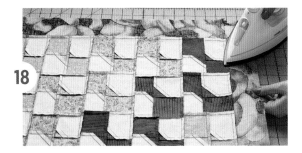

19 Cut the backing fabric and batting 4" (10 cm) longer and wider than the quilt top. Layer and baste the quilt (page 36). Attach a walking foot (page 11). Quilt by stitching the ditch (page 43), *following this sequence (p. 91)*: Begin with the center vertical seam; then the center horizontal seam. Then stitch in the ditch of the seam between the border and quilt top. Finish by stitching the remaining vertical seams between block rows and the remaining horizontal seams between block rows.

20 Bind the quilt, following the directions on page 44. Cut a piece of washed, unbleached muslin 6" (15 cm) long and the width of the quilt. Fold the short edges under ½" (1.3 cm) twice, and stitch a double-fold hem near the inner folded edge.

21 Fold the strip in half lengthwise, with right sides together and raw edges aligned. Stitch a ½" (1.3 cm) seam and press the seam allowances open. Turn the sleeve right side out; press it flat with the seam centered.

22 Pin the sleeve to the back of the quilt, close to the top edge and 1" (2.5 cm) from the sides. Slipstitch (page 62, step 13) the sleeve to the quilt along the upper and lower edges. Stitch through the backing and into the batting, but don't stitch through to the quilt top.

23 Insert a strip of sealed or painted wooden lath, cut ½" (1.3 cm) shorter than the width of the quilt, through the sleeve. Secure the lath to the wall by sliding the quilt aside and inserting nails or screws ½" (1.3 cm) from the ends of the lath.

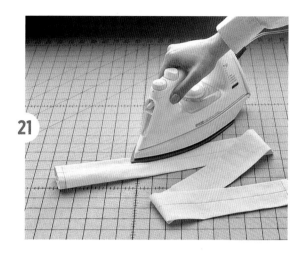

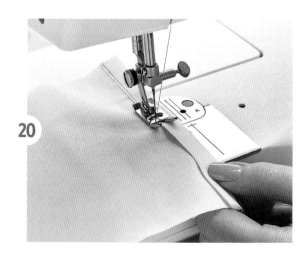

Glossary

Appliqué. This French word refers to a decoration or cutout that is applied to the surface of a larger piece of fabric. Many methods of appliqué are used, including simply machine stitching around the outline of the decoration or hand stitching invisibly.

Bias refers to the diagonal direction of a piece of fabric. True bias is at a 45 degree angle to both the lengthwise and crosswise grains. Woven fabric has the greatest amount of stretch on the bias.

Chainstitching. Sewing several individual seams without breaking the stitching threads between the pieces, thus saving time and trips to the ironing board.

Color Value refers to the relative lightness or darkness of a fabric. In selecting fabrics for a quilt project, it is often necessary to evaluate the color values of various fabrics, both solid colors and prints.

Crosswise Grain. On woven fabric, the crosswise grain runs perpendicular to the selvages. Fabric has slight "give" in the crosswise grain.

Double-fold hem. Hems that are made with two folds of equal depths, encasing the cut edge in the crease of the outer fold.

Fat quarters. A half-yard (0.5 m) of fabric, cut down the middle to measure 18" × 22" (46 × 56 cm). This is the equivalent of a quarter-yard (0.25 m) of fabric.

Finger-press. Rather than use an iron, seam allowances are temporarily pressed to one side with the fingers. This is usually done for bias seams to avoid distortion.

Finish. To improve the durability of a seam, the raw edge is secured with zigzag stitches that prevent raveling. This is important whenever narrow seam allowances are exposed and must withstand repeated handling or laundering.

Glue stick. This temporary fabric adhesive in a plastic tube is a convenient substitute for pinning or basting when you need to hold fabric in place temporarily before stitching. The glue can be applied in small dots. It won't discolor the fabric and can be washed out. It will not harm your machine or gum up your needle as you stitch.

Grainline. Woven fabrics have two grainlines. The lengthwise grainline runs parallel to the selvages. It is the strongest direction of the fabric with the least amount of "give." The crosswise grainline runs perpendicular to the selvages and will "give" slightly when pulled.

Lengthwise grain. On woven fabric, the lengthwise grain runs parallel to the selvages. It is the strongest direction of the fabric with the least amount of "give."

Line to the edge means that a fabric panel is backed with a lining that is cut to the exact same size. The two pieces are joined together by a seam around the outer edge; the seam allowances are encased between the layers.

Loft refers to the thickness and springiness of the batting.

Muslin. Often used for quilt backings and sleeves on wall hangings or for light background areas in patchwork quilts, this mediumweight, plain-weave cotton fabric is relatively inexpensive. Unbleached muslin is off-white with tiny brown flecks; bleached muslin is white.

Pivot. Perfect corners are stitched by stopping with the needle down in the fabric at the exact corner, before turning the fabric. To be sure the corner stitch locks, turn the handwheel until the needle goes all the way down and just begins to rise.

Pressing. This step is extremely important to the success of your quilting projects. Select the heat setting appropriate for your fabric and use steam. Lift and lower the iron in an overlapping pattern. Do not slide the iron down the seam, as this can cause the fabric to stretch out of shape, especially on the crosswise grain or bias.

Quilting hoop. Similar to an embroidery hoop, this circular or oval, two-piece wooden frame holds the quilt layers taut while you are hand-quilting. An adjustable screw allows you to tighten or loosen the outer hoop to accommodate various thicknesses without crushing the quilt.

Quilting template. A simple, rigid shape is used as a guide for tracing design lines onto the quilt top for machine or hand quilting. Templates can be cut from firm card stock or translucent vinyl. Ready-made vinyl templates and quilting stencils, also used for marking designs, can be purchased at quilt shops.

Sashing. Strips of fabric, plain or pieced, that are sewn between the square block units of a quilt.

Seam. Two pieces of fabric are placed right sides together and joined along the edge with stitches. After stitching, the raw edges are hidden on the inside, leaving a clean, smooth line on the outside.

Seam allowance. Excess fabric which lies between the stitching line and the raw edge. Stitching with a narrow ¼" (6 mm) seam allowance is traditional for quilting projects because it minimizes the bulk of fabric behind narrow strips and points.

Selvage. Characteristic of woven fabrics, this narrow, tightly woven outer edge should be cut away. Avoid the temptation to use it as one edge of a quilting piece, as it may cause seams to pucker and it may shrink excessively when washed.

Stitching in the ditch. An easy and often used quilting technique which gives definition to blocks, borders, and sashing. Place the quilt under the presser foot so the needle stitches between two fabrics and into the well of the seam.

Strip piecing. Creating pieced designs from long strips of fabric by stitching the strips together and then cutting them crosswise. This method saves time over cutting each piece individually and then sewing them together.

Temporary fabric adhesive. Available in a convenient spray can, this product eliminates the need for tedious hand basting. A light layer of this colorless adhesive holds the quilt top, batting, and backing layers together temporarily for machine or hand quilting. The adhesive will not gum up your needle. For some brands the adhesive simply diminishes after a few weeks. For others it can be removed by laundering.

Tension. When your machine puts the same amount of "pull" on both the top thread and the bobbin thread, your stitches lock exactly halfway between the top and bottom of the fabric layers. Even tension is essential for successful sewing. Some sewing machines require minor tension adjustments when switching from one fabric to another.

Zigzag stitch. In this setting, the needle alternately moves from left to right with each stitch. You can alter the width of the needle swing as well as the length of the stitch. A zigzag stitch that is twice as wide as it is long gives you a balanced stitch, appropriate for finishing the edge of a seam.

Patterns

To download these patterns for printing,
go to this link on our web site:

www.qbookshop.com/products/192622

Hand-appliquéd Zipper Bag, page 57

Quilt-as-you-go Christmas Stocking, page 65. Photocopy at 300%.

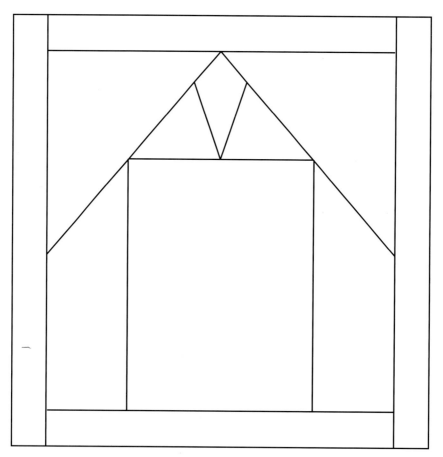

Paper-pieced Holiday Coasters, page 73

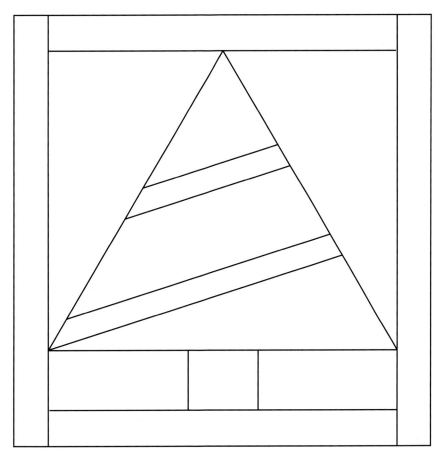

Paper-pieced Holiday Coasters, page 73

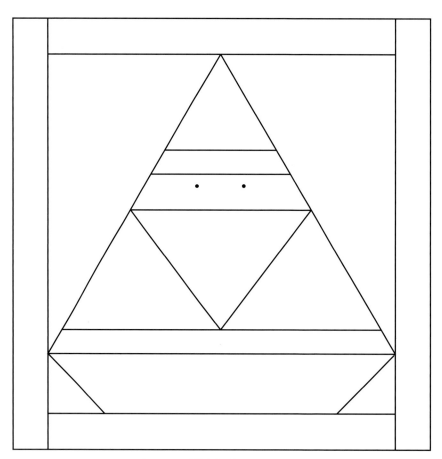

Paper-pieced Holiday Coasters, page 73

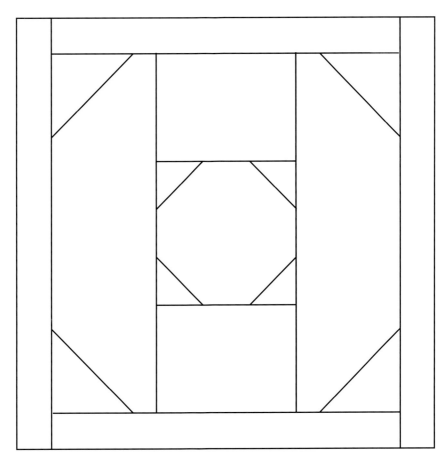

Paper-pieced Holiday Coasters, page 73

Index

A

Accessories, sewing machine, 10–11
Adjusting sewing machine
    tension, 16–17
Appliqué, 51, 57, 168
Appliquéd 1–55
Appliquéd zipper bag, 57–63
    patterns for, 170

B

Baby quilt, star sashing, 155–159
Balancing tension, 16
Basting, 36
    with glue, 53
Batting, 30–31
    for arranging quilt pieces, 158
Bias, 25, 168
Binding, 44
Blanket, doll, 147–153
Bobbins, 11
    winding, 13
Bow ties wall hanging, 161-167

C

Chainstitching, 123, 140, 149, 165, 168
Channel quilting, 43
Checkerboard placemats, 87–93
Christmas stocking, 65–71
Churn dash wall hanging, 139–145
Coasters, holiday, 73–79
    patterns for, 172–173
Color value tester, 29, 109
Connecting squares, 99
Crosswise grain, 25, 168
Cutting fabrics, 32–35
    tools for, 20–21, 32

D

Doll blanket, 147–153
Double-fold hem, 168

E

Edgestitching, 135

F

Fabric, 25–29
    backing, 27
    markers, 69
    preparing, 27
    straightening, 33
Fat quarters, 103, 168
Finger pressing, 67, 74
Flange pillow, 131–137
Flannel lap quilt, 111–115
Flying geese doll blanket, 147–153

G

Glossary, 168
Glue-baste, 53
Glue stick, 53, 168
Grainlines, 23, 25, 67, 168

H

Hand quilting, 41
Hanging quilts, 167
Holiday coasters, 73–79
Hook and loop tape, 135
Hot pad, appliqué, 51–55
How to use this book, 4–5

K

Knots, 41, 59

L

Lap quilt, flannel, 111–115
Lath, for hanging quilt, 167
Layering and basting, 36–39
Lengthwise grain, 25, 168
Lined to the edge, 147, 168
Loft, 31, 168
Log cabin sewing machine cover,
    123–129

M

Machine quilting, 42–43
Marking tools, 21
Mat for cutting, 21, 32
Measuring, 21
Muslin, 25, 169

N

Napkins, how to sew, 92
Needles,
    for hand quilting, 22
    sewing machine, 10, 12
Nine-patch pillow, 81–85

O

Ohio star flange pillow, 131–137
Outline quilting, 43

P

Paper-pieced holiday coasters, 73–79
    patterns for, 172–175
Patterns,
    for apple and leaf for zippered
        bag, 170
    for Christmas stocking, 171
    for holiday coasters, 172–175
Pieced sashing table runners,
    103–109
Pillow,
    doll bed, 153
    Ohio star flange, 131–137
    nine-patch, 81–85
Pins, 22
    inserting and removing, 47
Pivot, 175
Placemats, checkerboard, 87–93
Presser feet, 11
Pressing equipment and
    techniques, 23, 169

Q

Quilting hoop, 41, 169
Quilting techniques, basic, 40–43

R

Rail-fence wall hanging, 117–121
Rotary cutter and mat, 21, 30–35

S

Sashing, 95, 103, 111 140, 155, 169
Seam allowances, 18, 169
Seams, 18-19, 169
Selvages, 25, 33, 169
Sewing machine, 8–17
    accessories for, 10–11
    adjusting tension, 17
    balancing tension, 16
    bobbins, 11–13
    cover, 123–129
    inserting needle, 12
    parts, 8–13
    presser feet, 11
    threading, 14–15
    winding bobbin, 13
Sleeve, for hanging quilts, 167
Slipstitching, 62, 76, 85, 115
Squares, connecting, 99
Star sashing baby quilt, 155–159
Stitching diagonally, 101
Stitch-in-the-ditch quilting, 43, 169
Stocking, Christmas, 65–71
    pattern for, 171
Strip piecing, 111, 117, 169
Supplies, quilting, 20–23

T

Table runner, pieced sashing, 103–109
Table topper, double nine-patch,
    95–101
Temporary fabric adhesive, 61, 67, 76,
    150, 169
Tension, adjusting and
    balancing, 16–17
Thimble, 41
Thread jam, 19
Thread, types, 22
Threading sewing machine, 14–15
Tools, for quilting, 20–21

V

Value tester, for color, 29, 109

W

Wall hanging,
    bow ties, 161–167
    churn dash, 139–145
    rail-fence, 117–121
Winding bobbins, 13

Z

Zigzag stitch, 129, 169
Zipper, inserting, 61
Zippered bag, 57–63